Critical Guides to French Texts

37 Villon: Poems

D0230303

Critical Guides to French Texts

EDITED BY ROGER LITTLE, WOLFGANG VAN EMDEN, DAVID WILLIAMS

VILLON

Poems

John Fox

Professor of French
University of Exeter

Grant & Cutler Ltd
1984

© Grant & Cutler Ltd
1984
ISBN 0 7293 0185 0

I.S.B.N. 84-499-7261-2

DEPÓSITO LEGAL: V. 1.288 - 1984

Printed in Spain by
Artes Gráficas Soler, S.A., Valencia
for
GRANT & CUTLER LTD
11 BUCKINGHAM STREET, LONDON W.C.2

Contents

Preface

The italicized arabic numbers in brackets refer to works listed in the bibliography.

Designed as a close commentary on the best of Villon's poetry, and incorporating a literal translation, this study should ideally be used along with the French text. The best edition is by J. Rychner and A. Henry (*20*), but numbers of others are available and are described in the bibliography, as also are the most outstanding of the many recent studies of Villon and his poetry.

In the conclusion, modern interpretations of Villon, some of which have produced startling results, are assessed, as is Villon's relevance to our present day and age.

Introduction

France's greatest lyric poet ... This view of François Villon, put
forward by an eminent scholar, was not arrived at lightly (see *9*,
p.524). Rarely can so outstanding a reputation have rested on so
slender a foundation: slightly more than 3300 lines altogether,
falling into four categories: the *Lais* (sometimes called *Le Petit
Testament*), a short burlesque will of 320 lines written in 1456
when Villon was twenty-five; the *Testament* (sometimes called
Le Grand Testament), composed five years later, Villon's
longest poem, containing 2023 lines, a re-working of his earlier
theme after much hard experience and suffering; sixteen
miscellaneous poems, mostly ballades, usually assembled in
modern editions under the heading *Poésies diverses* or *Poèmes
variés*, composed over a number of years between 1456 and
1462; finally, eleven ballades in thieves' slang, often omitted
from even the principal editions, difficult to date, but composed
in all likelihood before 1460.

Despite its compactness, Villon's work is of uneven quality,
and it is to rather less than half of it that its fame is chiefly owed:
the first thousand lines of the *Testament*, several short passages
later in that work, and two ballades from the loosely knit
Poésies diverses. The purpose of the present study is to provide a
detailed analysis of these passages. The rest of Villon's output,
invariably vigorous and colourful even if less remarkable as lyric
poetry, is by no means neglected, but is not scrutinised so
closely. Biographical details are not given pride of place as they
so often are in commentaries on this poet's work, but are
brought in, briefly, when analysis of the text would become
obscure without them.

That Villon was writing only ten years before the introduction
of printing into France in 1470 explains why a mere four manuscripts have preserved his principal works, and one of these
contains only the *Lais*. The first printed version of his works

(referred to in most editions as I) dates from 1489. It was re-edited a number of times in the sixteenth century. Its exact source, which has not survived, does not appear to have given a particularly reliable version of Villon's text. Various revisions, in which no less a figure than Clément Marot had a hand, did little to improve matters. No surviving manuscript is altogether satisfactory, but one (fonds français 20041 of the Bibliothèque Nationale in Paris, usually referred to as ms C) gives the most complete and reliable text of Villon's works, the *Testament* in particular. Not until 1974 did an authoritative critical edition, based squarely on this manuscript, appear (*20*). Mentioned above, in the preface, it provides scholarly and informative notes on the text, and a careful analysis of the complex relationships between the manuscripts and the early printed editions. It has formed the basis of the present study. Not included, unfortunately, are the poems in thieves' slang, for which Lanly's edition (*18*) is the most reliable. Eclipsed at long last is the faithful Longnon-Foulet edition (*11*), first published in 1892 by August Longnon. Based ultimately on the 1489 edition, it was revised several times by Lucien Foulet (1914, 1923, 1932) in an altogether more scholarly manner than his sixteenth-century predecessors had managed. It provided the text of Villon's poetry for a number of other editions, some of which are still in print (for further details see bibliography). Textual variations amongst currently available editions are slight, although modernised forms and spelling (see *13*, *14*, *17*) sometimes involve considerable departures from the original.

1. Le Testament

I   In the year when I reached the age of thirty, when I had
drained the cup of my disgrace, neither entirely foolish nor
entirely wise, notwithstanding many sufferings undergone,
all of which I received at the hands of Thibault d'Aussigny
… if bishop he be, making the sign of the cross in the
streets, that he is any bishop of mine I deny.

The first line poses a problem for editors. The word-order is
unusual: not 'En l'an trentiesme de mon aage', but 'En l'an de
mon trentiesme aage', 'In the year of my thirtieth …'? In
Villon's day 'aage' can mean, not merely 'age', 'life', but also
'year'. This was pointed out long ago, but did not clarify
matters: 'Mais que signifierait "En l'an de ma trentième
année"?' asked Gaston Paris, doyen of medieval French studies
in the late nineteenth and early twentieth centuries (see *45*,
p.361). Considering it nonsensical, he suggested that Villon must
in fact have written 'En l'an trentiesme …' even though no
manuscript source, nor any early printed editions justify this
change, and no early commentator on Villon's *Testament* found
anything untoward in the original word-order of this line. The
revised order was often adopted, and is still followed in at least
one current edition (*17*). The most comprehensive edition of
Villon's works (*12*, II, p.79) suggests that both readings were
possible, the revised one being more usual. While this may
indeed be so, the unanimity of the fifteenth-century sources
must be respected, the more so as 'in the year of my thirtieth
year' is by no means nonsense, the reference being to the
calendar year in which Villon attained the age of thirty (modern
French would say 'l'année où j'ai eu mes trente ans'). Nowadays
even thirty may seem a very young age at which to plan for one's
death, but in Villon's day the average expectation of life was no
more than thirty. Although, then as now, the three-score years

and ten of the Bible represented a ripe old age, fewer people
attained it because of the prevalence of disease and the harshness
of living conditions.

What disgrace is referred to in the second line we cannot yet
know, but clearly the writer has been in trouble of some kind, to
what extent of his own making is never revealed; 'boire ses
hontes', 'to drink one's disgrace', is a sufficiently rare
expression for the suggestion to have been made more than once
that, in using it in a rondeau giving a condescending and unsym-
pathetic portrait of a down-and-out, the aristocratic prince-poet
Charles d'Orléans was referring to his contemporary, Villon.
Certainly the possibility is a real one, for there is evidence that
Villon sought the patronage of the duke a year or two before
writing the *Testament* (see *5*, II, pp.96-98 and *6*, pp.376-92) but
with little apparent success (see *29*, pp.45-46, *16*, I, p.49, *6*,
pp.376-92). In this context the third line is the equivalent of
'neither wholly guilty nor wholly innocent', a seemingly
objective, detached view of his own behaviour. At this juncture,
the fact that the first sentence is left incomplete gives difficulty.
'Nonobstant', 'notwithstanding', no doubt qualifies the preceding line, meaning that, like the common run of mortals, he is
neither altogether foolish nor altogether wise and that his
sufferings have not pushed him to either of these extremes. The
full meaning of lines 3-4 only emerges in the course of the next
few stanzas: his imprisonment has served no purpose. It has not
made a better man of him, nor has it, despite all the cruelty,
broken his spirit and driven him out of his mind. Line 4 is
unlikely to have been intended to lead on to the main clause
which in the event is never expressed, because, assuming that
this would have referred to the poet's intention to write a will
(cf. stanza X), it would have been something of a *non-sequitur*.
Tribulations are precisely what urge one to make a will; they are,
in this respect if in no other, an encouragement, not a hindrance.
And now the inevitable question: who was this Thibault
d'Aussigny, cause of all our author's woes? We must assume
that Villon was writing for a milieu which had knowledge of this
individual, and we for our part must turn to historical records.
We learn that he was Bishop of Orleans (cf. line 7) from 1452 to

1473, that history has not recorded him as an unjust or tyrannical figure (see *6*, pp.420-21), and that, faithful to the memory of Joan of Arc, he commemorated annually her liberation of Orleans.

The last two lines of this first stanza are a quite unexpected, and dramatic, veering-round, an abandoning of his first subject, himself, and of the seemingly dispassionate and detached air, the change being triggered off by the very mention of the bishop's name. Henceforth all attention is to be switched to Thibault d'Aussigny. Clearly the indignation Villon feels at the treatment meted out to him by the bishop is such that he cannot restrain himself, and his feelings have to come bursting out. What an impression of spontaneity is conveyed! It is as though the curtain rises after the first six lines have been spoken, and Villon appears suddenly before our eyes, giving vent to his pent-up emotions. But what, precisely, is the nature of this 'spontaneity' reflected in this sentence broken off half-way along its length, as happens in ordinary speech when some factor intervenes abruptly to interrupt the flow of thought? Is it really possible to be natural and spontaneous in lines of eight syllables, grouped together in stanzas of eight lines, each stanza having an intersecting rhyme pattern *a b a b b c b c*? And is it not significant that Villon's first surviving work, *Le Lais*, prototype of *Le Testament*, also begins with an incomplete sentence, or that a later stanza of the *Testament* (LXXX), heralded as the beginning of the testament proper, begins likewise, veering off at a tangent in its last two lines, leaving the first sentence hanging in the air? Clearly, however much Villon manages to convey the impression of having been caught out, and overwhelmed, by the strength of his feelings, this is a deliberate technique, an *artistic* spontaneity, no less effective for that, based on observation of ways in which people express themselves. Is this observation Villon's, and Villon's alone? Almost certainly not. It is known that he had been a student at the University of Paris and that he had taken his B.A. and M.A. there. This means that he had studied rhetoric, the art of persuasion, of using language in the manner most likely to enable one to achieve one's ends (see *5*, I, pp.36-49, *6*, pp.123-41). In medieval times students learned more how to be creative writers than critics, for the basis of literary studies was the use of language in the style of the various Latin classical authors rather than the writing of essays on these authors. The advantage lay in the encouragement given to creative writing, the disadvantage, paradoxically, in the casting of that writing in stereotyped patterns. However, it is not the intention here to digress from the text of the *Testament* in order to assess the relative merits of medieval and modern teaching of literature. Suffice to say that medieval rhetoric, like present-day stylistics though with a different motivation, drew attention to numbers of linguistic devices, amongst them anacoluthon, or *nominativus pendens*, a lack of grammatical sequence caused by a sudden substitution, under emotional pressure, of one subject for another. This is the device used so effectively by Villon in the first stanza of the *Testament*.

A quality greatly praised by medieval rhetoric — and this again is paradoxical in view of modern connotations of the term rhetoric — is brevity, of which an instance is provided in the expression in line 7 'signant les rues', which editors of the *Testament* invariably expand considerably in their explanations: 'bénissant la foule en faisant le signe de la croix', or 'faisant le signe de la croix sur la foule'. It is true that fifteenth-century French syntax was more conducive to brevity than is that of the twentieth century because it insisted less on the use and repetition of tool-words such as personal pronouns and prepositions, and was less concerned with grammatical logic, but on many an occasion we shall find Villon expressing a great deal in a few words, fewer even than his contemporaries would have needed.

Much of the flavour of Villon's poetry is present already in these opening lines of his major work. His style bears the influence of two elements: rhetoric, that is, studies of literary usage carried out in the class-rooms and lecture-rooms of his day, studies which themselves were a quintessence of observations made by the great writers of the past on the most effective ways possible of using language, and, arising from these studies, the poet's personal observations of the ways in which people express themselves. Villon's days as a student were some eight

years back at the time of writing the *Testament*, and his studies
had been absorbed, as it were, into the totality of his experience.
It is as though they had passed through the sieve of his
experience, constantly held in check by it and controlled in such
a way that his language never seems artificial or unduly literary
and never smacks openly of an acquired technique, of striving
after effect through the artificial application of a studied
dogma, which is the great failing of so much medieval French
verse. Villon is a past master at the art of making the contrived
appear natural. The object of rhetoric is persuasion, and we
shall be afforded many an opportunity of confirming that the
aim here is to persuade the reader that François Villon, 'ne du
tout fol, ne du tout saige', was by no means a villain, but one
whom others such as Thibault d'Aussigny, and life in general,
had treated with undue harshness. All writing in the first person
singular creates a literary 'persona' different from the real
author. Villon is no exception (scc *42*, pp.60-69), but his skill lies
in convincing us that the 'Je, François Villon ...' on the page in
front of us is the real person: we shall soon find that it is not so
much a matter of reading his text as of listening to him, arguing
with him, commiserating with him, philosophising with him on
the torments of the human condition. Resentment of harsh
treatment makes a clever beginning, quickly establishing a close
relationship with the reader, for while flattery can so easily be
feigned, indeed was so in those times when writers needed
patrons, personal resentment is far less likely to be mere
pretence or convention.

It takes Villon no fewer than five stanzas to exorcise his
feelings of hatred for the unfortunate bishop, balanced by a
further five expressing gratitude to the new King Louis XI,
(more accurately, four stanzas, since stanza X is an interpolation
(within an interpolation!) making no mention of the King),
feelings radically different, but given the circumstances, no less
heartfelt. Historical sources reveal that the King's chance
passage through Meung-sur-Loire on 2 October, 1461 on his
return from his coronation at Rheims on 15 August had been the
happy occasion of Villon's release (see stanza XI), along with
that of other prisoners. This information, combined with that

given in the first line of the *Testament*, suggèsts that Villon's thirtieth birthday occurred between 2 October 1461, and April 1462 (since the old style of reckoning began and ended the year in April).

Stanza II spells out more fully the nature of Villon's complaint against Thibault d'Aussigny:

> II He is not my lord nor my bishop, I hold no land beneath him, unless it be waste land. I owe him no faith and no homage with it. I'm neither his deer nor his hind. He fed me on a tiny loaf of bread and cold water a whole summer through. Generous or mean, to me he was very niggardly: May God be to him as he has been to me!

The last line of the first stanza is developed here: 'he is not a bishop who has any jurisdiction over me' — whereas the bishop of Paris would have had such jurisdiction, Villon having been brought up there and having spent his student days there, so belonging to the diocese of the capital. 'Soubz luy ne tiens' is a deviation from the syntactic norm 'De luy ...' in order to echo 'Soubz la main' of the first stanza. The reference to waste land is an emphatic way of saying 'I am not beholden to him in any way', leading to the marvellously effective line, with its spitting out of spiteful sibilants

> Je ne suis son serf ne sa biche.

Here again there are echoes of the rhetorical tradition, with its advocating of *annominatio*, a playing with words through use of homonyms, words with the same sounds but different meanings, hence 'serf' means 'serf', 'slave', but it also means 'deer' (spelling 'cerf') and this second meaning leads on to 'biche', literally 'hind', 'doe', though it is well attested in the sense of 'domestic animal' in the Middle Ages.[1]

---

[1] J. Dufournet sees in this line '... une nouvelle accusation contre l'évêque qui aurait des mœurs particulières et aimerait la compagnie de mignons', *29*, p.13. See too in greater detail (and more far-fetched), *31*, pp.17-28. The reader will have noticed that the translation given above is not unambiguous. The latest editors see no sexual innuendoes in this line, however: *20*B, pp.15-16. J. Favier comments rather cryptically: 'Entendons que Thibault d'Auxigny confondait les sexes', *6*, p.416.

While complaining bitterly about the meagre diet, and the harsh treatment meted out to him, Villon says nothing, here or later, about why the bishop imprisoned him in the first instance. Did he have Villon arrested merely on suspicion? Had he caught wind of Villon's participation, four or five years earlier, in the robbery of the Collège de Navarre in Paris? (See below, p.26). This is unlikely, since his obvious course of action would have been to turn Villon over to the authorities in the capital. There is a vague rumour — it hardly attains even to that status — that Villon had helped himself to the contents of the box for the poor and needy in the church of Meung-sur-Loire (see *5*, p.110, *7*, p.155). More recently, it has been suggested that Villon had joined a group of strolling players, an activity strictly forbidden to the clergy, and that, as a result, Thibault d'Aussigny had had him degraded, that is, stripped of the ecclesiastical status which he held as a University graduate, and imprisoned. Several recent works support the hypothesis that Villon had connections with the theatre (*25*, *6*, p.441, *8*, p.178, *27* passim), either as an actor, or as a writer of farces and *sotties*, or, like Molière after him, as a combination of both. It is clearly going too far, however, to see Villon as the author of most of the extant fifteenth-century French farces (*27*). Whether it will ever be demonstrated beyond all doubt that he wrote even a single one of them is doubtful, but what can be said is that the style of the *Testament* is at times reminiscent of theatrical techniques, particularly when the monologue threatens to become a dialogue, as is the case in stanzas III and IV:

III   And if anyone should wish to take me up on this and say that I am cursing him, I am not doing so, if I am understood properly. In nothing do I say any evil of him. Here is all the evil that I do have to say: If he has been merciful to me, may Jesus, King of Paradise, show him like mercy in soul and in body!

IV   And if he has been harsh and cruel to me, far more than I reveal here, I want the everlasting God to treat him according to the same reckoning. Yet the Church tells and

expects us to pray for our enemies! I tell you that,
whatever he has done to me, I have left it to God to decide
to whom the wrong and shame belong.

Here and on several subsequent occasions (stanzas XVIII-XIX,
XXXVI-XXXVII, LVIII-LIX, LXXI, LXXXII) Villon turns his
text into an argument, inventing an interlocutor who challenges
what he has just said and who is then answered in his turn. It is
clear, therefore, that as he writes Villon is measuring carefully
the likely effect of his words, anticipating readers' reactions and
answering them the moment they form: 'they'll say that I've
gone too far and that I'm cursing the bishop. I don't want more
trouble, so I'd better deny this even though I've no intention of
retracting anything'. Line 29 interjects an ironical objection, at
such a tangent to what has just been said in the preceding lines
that it seems to come not so much from Villon himself as a
prolongation of his wishes concerning the bishop, but from his
imagined opponent: 'I want the everlasting God to treat him
according to the same reckoning' — 'Yet the Church tells us and
expects us to pray for our enemies'. The 'vous' of line 31 is
unexpected, but better motivated with this interpretation: Villon
replies, as in the previous stanza, to his opponent, who stands
for you, the reader, whose criticism of Villon is disarmed at the
outset. The strength of Villon's conviction that he is in the right,
the bishop in the wrong, is conveyed by the bold declaration
with which stanza IV ends: 'let God decide who is really to
blame.'
      Stanzas V and VI conclude this first development:

V   And I shall pray for him sincerely, in the name of the
soul of the good late Cotart. But how? It will be from
memory since I'm lazy at reading. I'll make a Picart prayer
of it. If he doesn't know what that is, he'd better go and
find out, if he takes my word for it, before it's any later, at
Douai or Lille in Flanders!

VI   However, if he wants to hear a prayer said for him, by
the faith I owe my baptism, provided that he keeps the

secret, he will not fail in his expectation. I take in the
Psalter, since I am able to do, which is not bound in oxhide
or leather, the verse written the seventh of the psalm *Deus
laudem*.

The archives of Paris reveal that Jean Cotart was an attorney at
the ecclesiastical court in Paris who died in 1461, not long, therefore, before Villon wrote these lines. A later passage of the
Testament, stanza CXXV, suggests that he may have defended
Villon on at least one occasion. Villon calls him 'My attorney in
the ecclesiastical court', (line 1231). We have only Villon's word
for it that Cotart was fond of the bottle (later in the *Testament* a
whole ballade (lines 1238-1265) celebrates Cotart's drinking
prowess), but there is no reason to doubt this, so the association
of Cotart's name in Villon's prayers with that of the bishop is
hardly complimentary to the latter. Villon adds insult to injury.
The latter half of stanza V is obscure and has given rise to
several interpretations. What, in particular, was a 'Picard
prayer'? The most likely explanation is that the reference is to
the heretics in Picardy in Villon's day, some of whom, according
to chroniclers, had been burned at the stake as recently as May,
1460. These heretics believed in *silent* prayer or indeed no prayer
at all; that is what Villon's prayer for the bishop amounts to,
since 'par cueur' (line 35), meaning 'in imagination', was practi-
cally the equivalent of a negative: 'manger par cueur' really
meant not to eat at all. Advantageous also from Villon's point
of view was the fact that nobody can verify the contents of a
silent prayer. In the most unlikely event of the bishop taking up
the challenge and actually going to Picardy, it would no doubt
prove a wild goose-chase, the heresy having been eradicated by
the time he arrived. Finally, stanza VI, if the bishop insists on
hearing Villon's prayer, 'provided that he keeps the secret'[2]
Villon produces from his memory (his memory being the psalter
that has no leather binding) the seventh line of Psalm CVIII of
the Vulgate (Psalm CIX of the modern Bible): 'When he shall be

---

[2] But this line (43) is one of the most ambiguous in the entire work, and there are
several other possibilities: 'as long as I keep the secret', 'although I don't let
everyone know'; or 'crye' may by Villon's time be third person singular, present
indicative or subjunctive.

judged, let him be condemned: and let his prayer become sin'. Appropriate enough from Villon's point of view, less so however than the following line, the one Villon really intended in the view of most commentators: 'Let his days be few, and let another take his office'; the Latin version was even more fitting no doubt in Villon's eyes: 'et episcopatum eius alter accipiat', 'and may another occupy his bishopric'. (This same line is quoted by Peter with reference to Judas, Acts, I, 20.) Numbering of verses varied in medieval psalters and this may account for the difference, unless the error be attributed to Villon's memory, since he has just taken the precaution of warning us that he has not checked his reference ('I'm lazy at reading', line 36). Or, following the caution of the preceding stanzas, has he deliberately taken us as close as he dared to the verse he really intended, and left it to us to determine the true nature of his reference? — a successful manoeuvre, if so! It was, in any case, a fashionable scholarly mischief to find quotations in the psalms 'appropriate' for the various high and mighty ones of the day, church dignitaries in particular. One way and another, Villon has made his feelings about the bishop crystal clear despite the indirect and covert references. His revenge for those summer days spent languishing in prison has lived on down the ages.

Vituperation, not adulation, was Villon's forte: no court poet he. Hence the rather heavy-handed quality about the second development, beginning with stanza VII, in praise of his unwitting benefactor, King Louis XI. In this linking stanza Villon sends his prayer on its way accompanied by the fervent wish that it be received favourably by the 'son of God' with whose name he links firstly that of Our Lady, and secondly, as a climax to the stanza, that of the King himself. Stanzas VII, VIII and IX are closely associated in meaning, so much, indeed, that lines 49-69, as punctuated in the Rychner-Henry edition, constitute a single sentence:

> VII   And I pray to the blessed son of God whom I invoke
> in all my needs, that my humble prayer may be received by
> him, from whom I hold body and soul, who has preserved

me from many a blame and freed me from a vile power. May he be praised, and Our Lady, and Louis, the good King of France.

VIII   To whom may God give the happiness of Jacob, the honour and glory of Solomon (as for prowess, he has a great deal of that, strength too, upon my soul, in truth); in this transitory world, in all its length and breadth, in order that he be remembered, may God grant that he live as long as Methuselah.

IX   And may he see[3] twelve fine children, all male, of his precious royal blood, as brave as was the great Charles, conceived in wedlock, as courageous as was Saint Martial. Thus may it be with the late dauphin! I wish him no other ill, and then Paradise at the end.

The prayer of stanza VII is no doubt that of the preceding stanza, although the changed context, now that the figure of the bishop is receding from view, gives it a new dimension: along with Villon's wishes for the bishop goes his thankfulness at being released from prison, and it is this thankfulness which now assumes precedence and motivates these three stanzas. This diptych which paints the bishop as a tyrant, the King as a benefactor, does not have the support of history, which would reverse these descriptions, (Louis XI, 'the spider King', is the originator of the infamous iron cages in which prisoners were kept in his dungeon at Loches), but there is nothing impartial about Villon's pronouncements: he presents people according to the roles they have played in his life. The broader patterns of history are no concern of his. The 'happiness of Jacob' (line 57), explained at the beginning of the following stanza, is that he had twelve sons, the 'honour and glory' of Solomon no doubt refer to his legendary wisdom, the length of Methuselah's life, to be that of Louis XI's also, was 'nine hundred sixty and nine years' according to the Book of Genesis (5, 27), the great Charles was of course Charlemagne, and Saint Martial, first bishop of

---

[3] 'See' (the infinitive 'veoir' rather than the adverb 'voire' of other manuscripts) reflects biblical wording, cf. Book of Job, 42, 16.

Limoges in the third century, seems to be chosen here for the implication of his warlike name. Such a cornucopia of blessings all this, not to be wondered at, however, in the circumstances. Villon clearly felt that he owed, not just his freedom, but his very life, to the King, and needed, in any case, to build the King up in opposition to the bishop, a hint possibly to the reader that he was in the King's favour — no need to give the true circumstances!

This first wave of emotion, the indignation and the gratitude alike, is now almost spent, and Villon reverts to the subject with which he had begun: himself:

> X   And since I am feeling weak, far more in wealth than health, as long as I am in full possession of my wits, the few that God has lent me, for I have not borrowed them from anybody else, I have written this long-lasting testament, by my last will, this one alone and irrevocable.

Here at last is the material which presumably could have completed the main sentence of stanza I: 'while still in full possession of my wits I have written this testament by my last will.' Noteworthy is the parody of the conventional terminology of wills in two joking asides (lines 74 and 77) which are interruptions to what is already an interpolation (all stanza X) within a much longer interruption (lines 7-88) which divides, as we have seen, into two main sections! This uneven, parenthetical, Chinese-box-like structure contributes, like the unfinished beginning of stanza I, to the impression of spontaneity. We are made to feel that this is not a literary composition, but a man talking directly to us, arguing his case, putting in the occasional pleasantry in order to lighten the mixture. After the usual declaration by the testator that he is feeling weak, he adds jestingly (line 74): 'more as regards wealth than health', and having referred, as was common in wills of the period, to the few wits that God has lent him, he slips in the aside (line 77): 'for I have not borrowed them from anybody else'. How seriously is the reader meant to take all this? For the moment he is left wondering, but enough strength of feeling has been revealed in the opening stanzas, and enough physical hardship evoked, to show that this is not just one more of the fashionable light-hearted and burlesque strings of legacies ('I leave my shoes to the cobbler, my hair-clippings to the barber' etc.) to which the author, as a later stanza (LXXV) informs us, had turned his hand back in 1456 (a reference to *Le Lais*). Joking may linger on in the occasional aside, but it is no longer the principal motivation.

Villon has not quite finished showering blessings on the King. The reader must have become accustomed by this time to a good deal of surface untidiness and apparent disjointedness, while the single-mindedness of the author's underlying intention to justify himself and present himself in the most favourable light possible has not yet been fully revealed:

> XI   I wrote it in the year '61, when the King freed me
> from the grim prison of Meung and gave me back my life,
> as a result of which, for as long as I live [lit. my heart
> lives], I shall be beholden to him, and shall be until I die.
> Good deeds must not be forgotten.

While Villon's hatred of the bishop had to be explained at the outset in order not to appear gratuitous and unjustified, his adulation of the monarch — which all loyal subjects were in duty bound to echo — finds full explanation only at this late juncture. So far we have been told that it was Christ who freed him from 'a vile power' (line 54) and only now do we learn — what it was easy enough to guess from the end of stanza VII onwards — that King Louis had been the actual agent who put Villon's liberation into effect. Historical records, as we have seen (above, p.15), corroborate what Villon tells us in the first half of this stanza. Grammatically 'il mourra' of line 87 can refer either to the King, or to Villon ('il' = 'mon cœur'). Since Villon has just hinted at his own approaching end (line 73), and has fervently wished for the King a life extending far ahead into the remote future, it clearly suits the spirit of the passage to follow the second possibility. There was a tendency in Villon's time to round a stanza off with a proverb or proverbial-type expression (see *8*, ch.II). He is skilled at coining apophthegmatic lines with all the pithiness of a proverb, and this he has done in line 88.

With stanza XII we move into a new phase. The changing sequences of the opening stanzas, moving from Villon to the bishop, then from the bishop to the King, back again to Villon and to the King, are now over. Villon begins to describe his experiences, always in general tones, and in a broader context than hitherto, not just over the preceding months. The justification for this development, if one were needed, would no doubt be that reminiscences of one's life are quite suitable introductory material for a will, which is a kind of summing-up, even though such reminiscences are a good deal more extensive in Villon's literary work than in most examples of the real thing. The simple truth is that the formula gave Villon the right to speak about himself in his own way, and provided him with a marvellous excuse: a dying man has the right to say whatever he chooses (line 728). The more he rambles amongst his memories, the greater the impression of authenticity. Just how ill he was in reality on his release from the prison at Meung-sur-Loire, is not known, but his physical hardship does not seem to have begun with his imprisonment:

> XII   Now it is true that after lamentations and tears and anguished moanings, after sadness and grief, toil and painful wanderings, suffering opened up for me my fickle mind, as sharp as a ball, more than did all the commentaries of Averroes on Aristotle.

Experience of life has taught him more than university studies. The commentaries on Aristotle, to which he alludes, by the twelfth-century Hispano-Arabian philosopher Averroes, were a well-known 'prescribed text' in the university curriculum of Villon's day (see 6, p.58). Such studies had done little to mature his 'lubres sentemens' (lit. 'shifting', or 'uncertain', thoughts), as sharp as a ball, not sharp at all that is, obtuse in the literal and extended meanings of the term. Indeed, both influences, university training on the one hand, the harsh realities of his existence on the other, may be discerned throughout the *Testament* (see above, p.13). But what do we learn here about these harsh realities? The first four lines of stanza XII pile up the abstractions; the very accumulation, along with the matching sound patterns ('*pl*ains et *pl*eurs', 'angoi*ss*eux gemi*ss*emens') underlines the intensity of the suffering, but to what, precisely, does Villon refer? It could be to his imprisonment once more were it not for the last and most revealing of these expressions: 'griefz cheminemens' on which he expands in the next stanza, using the same word in verbal form:

> XIII   Even at the height of my troubles, travelling along penniless [lit. without heads or tails], God, who comforted the pilgrims of Emmaus according to the Gospels, showed me a good town and provided me with the gift of hope. However vile the sinner may be, God hates nothing but perseverance in sin.

The 'bonne ville' to which his wanderings brought him is thought to have been Moulins, seat of the dukes of Bourbon, whose device (see line 102) was 'Esperance'; in just the same way the Saviour had given hope to the despairing 'pilgrims' at Emmaus (Luke, 24, 13-53). In a collection of sixteen short poems by Villon, most of them ballades (see below, p.92), there is one addressed to the Duke of Bourbon begging for financial assistance and referring to its author in terms similar to those used in stanza XII of the *Testament* (see *20*C, p.50, lines 3-4):

> François Villon, que Travail a dompté
> A coups orbes ...

> (François Villon, whom suffering has overcome with mighty blows ...)

Our poet appears to have been travelling (the word is appropriate, deriving as it does from French 'travail') through Northern France in search of a literary patron, and may have found a temporary haven with the Duke of Bourbon (see *6*, pp.430-34). But the moment has come for us to turn aside from the poetry to ask what is known from other sources about Villon's life prior to that fateful summer of 1461.

The Paris archives reveal that, three years after graduating there in 1452 (see above, p.13) Villon killed a priest in the Latin Quarter. There were no witnesses to their fight with daggers. The long, vivid account (see *6*, pp.193-98) provided to the authorities, still on record, is entirely Villon's: the priest had started the quarrel and dealt the first blow. After stabbing him in the groin, Villon at first ran away, 'fearing the severity of justice', but then applied for letters of pardon, and was successful. One detail that may throw light on Villon's life at the time: he is referred to in these documents under two names: François des Loges and François Villon. It is further recorded that, when he went to have his wounds dressed, he gave a third name: Michel Mouton, while other sources reveal that he was known under yet another name, perhaps the original one: François de Monterbier, a corruption possibly of Montcorbier.

Shortly before Christmas of the following year, Villon wrote the first of his two testaments, the *Lais*, prototype for his main work five years later. He is leaving Paris for Angers, he says, because he has been crossed in love. The 'amant martyr', we are bound to note, was a fashionable literary hero of the day. After a series of joking legacies, he tells us that, sitting alone in his cold room that evening, he heard the Sorbonne bell strike nine, stopped work to say his prayers, and fell after that into a trance, waking up to find his ink frozen and the candle-flame extinguished. But what was the nature of this strange trance? The archives reveal that, on 24 December 1456, Villon took part in a robbery at the Collège de Navarre, largest and richest of the colleges that made up the University of Paris. Had he and his confederates agreed to assemble on hearing the Angelus bell strike nine? Was this the start of the robbery? Strange trance indeed if so (see *26*)! They got away with 500 gold crowns, of which Villon's share was 120. The *Lais*, as we have seen, tells us that Villon was leaving for Angers because of an unhappy love affair. He told his fellow-thieves a different story: he had a wealthy uncle there and was going to spy out the land... It is conjectured, however, that his real motive in leaving was to turn over a new leaf and to try to get himself established as a court poet somewhere in the provinces (see *26*, also *20*D, pp.13-14). While one of his poems is addressed to the Duke of Bourbon, two others concern that even more promising patron, referred to above (see p.12), Charles, Duke of Orleans, one of the most distinguished poets of the age. It was while Villon was away, barely six months after his departure (in fact in May, 1457) that one of his confederates, Guy Tabarie (ironically referred to in the *Testament* as a 'truthful man', line 860), drank too much in the *Pomme de Pin*, one of the numerous taverns of Paris, and was heard boasting about his part in the robbery. Subsequently, helped on by a little torture, he revealed the whole story down to the smallest details (see *6*, pp.336-42). Villon knew about this (cf. his reference to Tabarie) and as a result kept away from Paris, longer probably than he had intended.

After his release from imprisonment, at the time of writing the *Testament*, his position remained desperate, for if he returned to Paris, it would be prison for him again. A reference in one stanza suggests that the *Testament* was written while he was in hiding not far from the capital (stanza CIII: 'If Robin Turgis [a Paris innkeeper] comes to see me, I'll pay him for his wine, but if he finds out where I'm living he's cleverer than a divine ...'). It was essential that in the *Testament* Villon should present himself in the most favourable light possible, since his troubles were by no means over. This is no doubt the driving force behind the first half of the *Testament*, even though it eventually rises far above the tawdry circumstances which gave it birth: the need to gain some sympathy for himself, to show that he was not such a bad fellow after all, and a notable poet to boot. He knew that, if he returned to Paris, even the most lenient treatment would involve returning his share of the stolen money, and this he could not manage without the help of friends and relatives. Particularly important in this respect (ironical though this must seem) were the clergy of the Latin Quarter, Villon's only true home. One of these, Guillaume de Villon, chaplain at the church of Saint-Benoît-le-Bientourné, was his benefactor and had made possible his university studies. Our poet took his pen-name from the chaplain to whom he refers in the *Testament* as 'my more than father' (line 849). It was quite likely in order to please the chaplain and such as he that Villon placed a number of biblical allusions in the *Testament* and confessed freely (stanzas XII-XVI) that he was a sinner. He did in fact return to Paris, preceded in all likelihood by the *Testament*, the promise to restore the necessary sum was duly made, and Villon allowed to go free, only to be condemned shortly afterwards to death, a sentence commuted on appeal to ten years' exile from Paris, on account of a street brawl in which he seems to have been no more than a bystander (see *6*, pp.490-93). Early in 1463 he departed from Paris, and from history. Nothing more is known about him, though his later years are the subject of more than one piece of fantasy in the works of Rabelais, suggesting that, already in his day, Villon's end was a subject for conjecture.

Although it would have been possible to continue this textual commentary on Villon's major work without reference to this extraneous information, it none the less gives us deeper insight into this most partial and reticent of self-confessions. Many of the contemporaries for whom the *Testament* was primarily intended possessed this information anyway, and without it it would have been difficult to understand why, from the end of stanza XIII onwards, Villon is so keen to apologise for and explain away (always avoiding details) his wrongdoing. Clearly there is something he prefers to refer to only indirectly, and now we know what it was: not so much his quarrel with the priest, for which he could claim self-defence, but the robbery in which he had participated, and perhaps other adventures of this kind, for it is clear that he had become involved in the Paris underworld (he is the author, besides, of several ballades in thieves' jargon, see *14*, *17*, *18*, *19*, *21*). It is no surprise that reflections on his wrongdoing should appear at this juncture. Villon is engaged in a practice that has already occurred in the *Testament* and will occur again: he is anticipating charges levelled against him and attempting to answer and disarm them at the outset, hence the beginning of the next stanza, which says in effect, 'Yes, I know I'm a sinner, but ...' After the heavy insistence on his tribulations, this is a *non-sequitur* which makes sense only if it relates, not to what is expressed, but to what is suppressed:

XIV   I am a sinner, I know it well, yet God does not wish
for my death, but that I should be converted and live righteously, as any other consumed by sin. Although I may be
dead in sin, God is alive, and His mercy, if conscience gives
me remorse, through His grace grants me pardon.

Good Christian dogma, this, with which the Church authorities,
even a Thibault d'Aussigny, could hardly disagree: 'As I live,
saith the Lord God, I have no pleasure in the death of the
wicked; but that the wicked turn from his way and live...'
(Ezekiel, 33, 11). Many other quotations from the Bible could be
produced in support of Villon's arguments. Hence what alone is
essential is remorse, Villon asserts — a powerful argument in
making out a case for himself, even though his own repentance
is implicit rather than explicit. A point of language in line 107: it
would be necessary in modern French to write: 'que je me
convertisse', and preferable, though not essential, to continue:
'et que je vive en bien'. Even in the fifteenth century it would be
more normal to provide the direct object pronoun before
'convertisse', and here as elsewhere the wording is the most
laconic and concentrated that fifteenth-century syntax would
allow. Remarkable also are the balance and contrast of phraseology. Twice in this stanza there is a strongly drawn death-life
opposition, in lines 106-07 and 109-10; on the second occasion
the sharply etched monosyllables 'Dieu vit' stand out from their
context, the sense pause after 'vit' contributing to this effect.
   The following stanza seeks confirmation of this train of
thought in a secular framework, referring to what was
undoubtedly seen then as the outstanding vernacular work of
Northern France, the *Roman de la Rose*:

XV   And as the noble *Roman de la Rose* says and affirms
in its opening lines, that one must forgive a youthful heart
its follies when it is seen in the ripeness of old age, alas! it
speaks the truth. Those, then, who press so hard upon me,
would not wish to see me reach maturity.

Villon's memory is at fault, his reading days, as he has told us,

being far behind him: he names the main work by Jean de Meun
but is actually quoting from a lesser known one by the same
author, appropriately enough his literary *Testament*. The lines
must have lingered in his mind since he gives two exact quotations:

> Bien doit estre escusé *jone cuer en jonesse*
> Quant Diex li done grace d'estre *viel en viellesce*. (see *20*B,
> pp.28-29)

The note of self-pity increases in the concluding lines, and the
plural, 'those who press so hard upon me ...' reveals (what the
historical documents referred to above confirm) that he had
made other enemies apart from the Bishop of Orleans.

Stanza XVI develops further this self-justification:

> XVI   If, by my death, the public good would benefit in
> any way, I should sentence myself to die like an iniquitous
> man, so help me God! I do no harm to young or old,
> whether I'm on my feet or in my coffin. The hills don't
> move from their places, one way or another, for a poor
> man.

But we know, as numbers of Villon's fellow-Parisians knew,
that he had killed a priest, robbed a college and was possibly
guilty of other misdemeanours (Thibault d'Aussigny certainly
thought so!), so how are we to take all this? Is it simply a clever
'front' designed to get its author out of a sticky situation? A wily
piece of self-defence constructed on a foundation of hypocrisy?
Or did Villon believe sincerely in what he was saying?
'Sincerity', it must be admitted, is an outmoded literary term, a
concept made fashionable by the nineteenth-century Romantic
movement (see *24*). It is impossible, we are assured nowadays, to
make any valid pronouncement on what, precisely, is going on
in an author's mind when he sets pen to paper, on his exact
relationship with his text, on his degree of involvement in it.
Speculation on the author's true feelings is mere embroidery, an
irrelevance. Even when all this is conceded, it remains that

Villon's poetry, whatever his true convictions, is so intensely subjective that the reader inevitably wonders about its degree of authenticity (to use a term more acceptable to critics in the late twentieth century) and ponders on probabilities. The reader's reactions to Villon's poetry will very likely be influenced by the result of such reflections. When he says that the bishop treated him harshly, surely he believed this? He remains reticent about his crime, and does not protest his innocence, complaining only of the cruel treatment he received and of the Bishop of Orlean's wrongfully claiming jurisdiction over him. That he was indebted to the King, he surely believed; that he had suffered hardship in the course of his wanderings (how long he was able to live off the proceeds of the robbery we can only guess), that Christianity would condemn him only for persistence in wrongdoing, not for past wrongdoings for which (he implies) he repents; that his life — like that of other poor men — was of trifling significance, doing no harm to anyone (the killing of the priest, as the authorities had accepted, had been self-defence; the robbery had not even been noticed for two months). In the ensuing stanzas Villon will develop this plea further, and the probabilities are vastly in favour of the literary 'persona' being, at times, close to the real author's view of himself, even though it is to a large extent an exercise in self-justification.

Authenticity is further revealed in a particular obsession which makes its first appearance in stanza XIV: whatever his misdemeanours, he has done nothing to deserve being sentenced to death. Lines 106 and 121 both refer cryptically to 'ma mort', not in the sense of death by natural causes, the anticipation of which motivates most wills, but in the sense of death as a punishment. Had he in fact had to face the death penalty at some stage? One of the poems concerning the court of Blois appears to suggest this: referring to the birth of Marie d'Orléans, the duke's daughter (19 December 1457), Villon writes:

... I would have been a dead creature, had it not been for your gentle birth... (See *20C*, p.43, lines 74-75)

Does this refer to some real happening, the princess's birth

serving the miraculous purpose that the King's passing through
Meung-sur-Loire was to do four years later, or is it simply poetic
hyperbole?[4] Hyperbole obviously does motivate the famous
Ballade des pendus in which Villon goes a step further,
imagining the death sentence to have been actually carried out
on him: this last despairing plea for understanding and forgiveness comes from his corpse as it swings on the gallows at the
mercy of the wind (see p.96). This ballade is commonly
supposed to have been written after the *Testament* but of this
there is no proof: 'Rien ne permet d'assigner une date à la
composition de cette ballade' (*20*D, p.110). That he actually was
sentenced to death, after his return to Paris at the end of 1462,
may seem a supreme irony, the more so as the cause was not the
robbery but a street-brawl in which, as we have seen (above
p.28), Villon had been no more than a bystander. The cruelty
and fickleness of justice in those time, the incorrigibility of
Villon's nature, which even the *Testament* cannot conceal
altogether, the harshness of his 'Fortune' (a subject soon to be
developed at length) made a dangerous and unpredictable
mixture, as well he knew. That he was for long haunted by this
fear does not seem so unnatural, the more so in the particular
circumstances in which the *Testament* was composed.
Significant in this respect are lines 119-20 which suggest that in
some quarters it was being vigorously argued that Villon should
be put to death; at least one other member of the gang that had
robbed the Collège de Navarre, Colin Cayeux, had been
executed, in 1460, not long before the *Testament* was written.
The anxieties, preoccupations, regrets that Villon expresses in
his lyrical self-analysis are obviously real enough, even though
there is clearly some concealment of misdeeds and partiality in
the judgment of others and of himself, but in these very
imperfections, in the differences between society's view of him
and his own view, is the most powerful indication that we have
of Villon's authenticity, and, paradoxically, of his right to
speak, in some measure at least, for all individuals, particularly,

---

[4] The latest editors think that the passage refers to 'un état de complet dénue-
ment' and to nothing else (*20*D, p.62), while Favier thinks that Villon was saved
from the hangman's noose, *6*, p.389.

but not solely, those out of step with the society in which they live. Villon is everyman's outsider. We none of us possess the gift of seeing ourselves as others see us, and perhaps even Robert Burns would have admitted, on reflection, that it is just as well that we do not. Let us have a catechismal conclusion on this central issue. Question: Is this the real Villon? Answer: No. Question: Is this Villon as he saw himself? Answer: With certain reticences, and some self-delusion, possibly so. Question: Is this Villon as he would like his readers to see him? Answer: Yes, of course.

In stanzas XVII-XXI, though increasingly concerned with his self-defence, Villon stands aside for a moment in order to allow the first of several surrogates to take his place, one who, significantly enough, had been threatened at a crucial stage in his life with the death penalty:

XVII   At the time when Alexander reigned, a man called Diomedes was brought before him, tied up (fingers and thumbs) like a thief, for he was one of those pirates we see roving the seas. And he was placed before this captain to be sentenced to death.

XVIII   The emperor thus addressed him: "Why are you a robber on the seas?" The other gave him this reply: "Why do you call me a robber? Because you see me roaming the seas in a tiny craft? If like you I could arm myself, like you I should be emperor.

XIX   But what can you expect? From my fate, against which I can do nothing effective, which treats me so falsely, comes all this way of life. Excuse me a little, and know that in great poverty — this is a common saying — there lies no great loyalty."

XX   When the emperor had listened carefully to all that Diomedes had to say "Your fortune I shall change for you, from bad to good" he said. This he did. Never afterwards did Diomedes say a cross word to anyone, but remained a loyal man. Valerius gives this for the truth, he who was called the Great in Rome.

XXI   If God had allowed me to meet some other merciful
Alexander who had brought happiness to me and if I had
then been seen to stoop to crime, I should sentence myself
with my own voice to be burned and put to ashes.
Necessity makes people take to crime, and hunger makes
the wolf come out of the woods.

Diomedes, it need hardly be said, represents Villon, and it is
noteworthy that stanza XIX is so arranged that it could be a plea
addressed by Villon on his own behalf directly to the reader.
Those elements which identify the speaker as Diomedes the
pirate are all contained in the last five lines of the preceding
stanza; every single utterance of stanza XIX could come straight
from Villon to the reader of his poetry. A separate ballade, the
Débat de Villon et de son cœur (see below p.93), in which he
tries to justify his conduct in the face of a nagging conscience,
makes the same excuse: fate had decreed that his life should be
so, he had never had a chance, and there was nothing he could
do about it. Once again the death penalty casts its shadow across
Villon's verse: if I had encountered a merciful Alexander and
had subsequently committed a crime, I would have sentenced
myself to death. A luckless individual driven by force of circumstances deserves a more lenient and considerate judgment —
such is the clear implication, such the fervent plea made by
François Villon after release from imprisonment and before
emerging from hiding to face the consequences of his part in the
robbery of the Collège de Navarre. Self-interest drives Villon to
reinforce his case by referring on three occasions to poverty in
general terms, each time as a climax to a stanza, a plea, therefore, with a strongly Christian bias: lines 127-28, 150-52, 167-68.
The last of these lines, which concludes the Alexander-Diomedes
exemplum, is a mere figure of speech today, but was a telling
remark in those times when packs of wolves actually did invade
the outskirts of Paris and carried off children. Based squarely on
his own case though it is, Villon's argument is a compulsive one
and carries a modern ring about it: do not blame the wrongdoer,
blame the conditions in which he has had to live.[5]

[5] Villon has again got his source wrong. The story of Alexander and the pirate

Stanza XXI heralds the beginning of a long passage of twenty stanzas containing some of the finest of Villon's lyric poetry, a passage full of nostalgia and regrets, looking back over his past, giving the impression that he is musing with himself, though he never ceases angling for the sympathy and support of others (notice in particular the last sentence of stanza XXIII):

> XXII   I look back with regret to the time of my youth (when I enjoyed myself more than the next man up to the threshold of old age) which has hidden its departure from me. It went away not on foot, not on horse. Alas! how then? It has flown suddenly off, and left me no gift.

> XXIII   It has gone, and I remain poor in sense and knowledge, sad, disheartened, blacker in mood than a blackberry, without rent, income, possessions. The least of my relatives, I tell the truth, hastens to disown me, forgetting natural duty for want of a little cash.

Clearly, these stanzas are still concerned with self-justification, but the tone is becoming less argumentative, more sentimental, 'Je plains' having a stronger meaning than in modern French, the equivalent of 'Je regrette amèrement' (see *20*B, p.33), and the picturesque metaphor on the swift departure of youth having an emotional impact all the greater in that it is surely an impression shared by many as they look back on their early years. Henceforth, as stanza succeeds stanza, a gradual and subtle transformation takes place in the literary 'persona': Villon the individual, concerned with his reactions for and against those who have closely affected his life, gives way to Villon the common man, prey to nostalgia, to the torment of hindsight, to the remembrance of friends once so close, now vanished forever, to fears of poverty, disgust with old age, horror of death. If the early arguments did not win the reader over, we cannot avoid becoming enmeshed in this finely woven net of emotions, because they are emotions which are part and

---

Dionides does not appear in the works of Valerius Maximus. There are several possible sources, including John of Salisbury. Other writers of the times make the same mistake.

parcel of human existence. Villon's literary 'persona' becomes a
spokesman for the common man. It would be an unimaginative
and hard-hearted person indeed who could read these stanzas
and remain unaffected by them. The orchestration is subtle and
complex, moving forward on different levels simultaneously, for
even the soaring flights of lyric nostalgia are apt to contain
passing references to his own wretched plight, persistent
reminders of the work's ultimate source. Stanza XXIII is
concerned with his destitution and possibly something more
than that: 'for want of a little cash' could well be, not simply a
reminder of his poverty, but a veiled allusion to that
misdemeanour whose consequences had still to be faced, the
robbery of the Collège de Navarre, a clever way of saying: was it
really all that serious a crime? Does it really merit punishment?
And a hint besides to his relatives that they might reasonably be
expected to help him find the money — which in the event they
no doubt did (see above, p.28).

> XXIV   And I have no fear of having spent anything on
> fine food or sensual pleasures. I have sold nothing through
> too much love-making that anyone can reproach me with,
> nothing at least, that costs them very much. I say this and
> believe it to be the truth; I can defend myself against such
> charges: he who has done no wrong must not say that he
> has.

> XXV   Very true it is that I have loved, and would love
> willingly, but a sad heart and a famished belly not a third
> satisfied keep me from the paths of love. After all, let him
> make up for this who has eaten and drunk his fill, for the
> dance comes from the belly.

Here the note of self-justification wells up ever more strongly in
yet another gloss on the theme of the opening stanzas: 'I may
not be wholly innocent, but I am not a wastrel.' Self-analysis is
not going to lead Villon to unwarranted self-reproach. Stanza
XXV, 'Bien est verté ... Mais ...', is another qualified confession, one that he was quite confident would not shock; (many

men, even those of highest renown, had made fools of themselves because of love, as Villon gleefully and lengthily points out in the *Double Ballade*, lines 625-72). Hence the follow-up: he would love again if circumstances permitted, but of this he sees no chance. His own deprivation, of which he reminds us from time to time (cf. lines 828, 842-43) does not stop him from giving a wry salute to those luckier than he, but these lines (198-200) are more than that, they are also a jarring hint to those well-fed members of court circles who idealised love in their elegantly turned rondels that its basis in fact is a solidly materialistic one: your fine affections depend on a full belly.

> XXVI   I know[6] full well that, had I only studied in the time of my foolish youth and given myself to good habits, I should have a house and a soft bed. But what did I do? I fled from school as does the naughty child. As I write these words, my heart is near to breaking.

Stanza XXVI does not actually conjure up one of Villon's finger-wagging interlocutors (cf. III) but clearly rehearses the sort of reproach that would be made to him by his elders and betters on his return to the capital. Even though he was no doubt calculating his effects, there is clearly no reason to doubt the strength of his feelings. He naturally regretted his destitution, and acknowledged that to some extent it was of his own making. To his contemporaries familiar with his misdemeanours, of which the Paris archives afford us a glimpse, this must have seemed obvious. As well, therefore, from Villon's point of view, to concede the truth of this. But avowals of misbehaviour are eked out with interludes of self-justification in a subtly balanced mixture. It is all expressed already in the third line of the *Testament*: 'Not entirely foolish, not entirely wise.' In stanza XXVI we are at the heart of Villon's confessions. These are the blackest charges that he is prepared to lay at his own door. The 'temps de ma jeunesse' (cf. line 169) acquires a new and signifi-

---

[6] 'Bien sçay...', the reading of C, the most reliable manuscript, is preferred to the more usually accepted version 'Hé Dieu ...' because it fits far better the argumentative, rather than simply emotional, nature of the passage (see *20*B, p.37).

cant adjective: 'folle'. Villon projects a sort of 'prodigal son' image, and perhaps hoped to evoke memories of that parable in the religious milieu of the Latin Quarter, particularly in one of its distinguished members, his 'more than father' (line 849) Guillaume de Villon.

> XXVII   I interpreted too much in my heart's favour the Sage's saying (much good will it do me now!) which said: "Rejoice, my son, in your youth", but elsewhere he serves a very different dish, for here is what he says, no more and no less: "Childhood and youth are nothing but excess and ignorance".

> XXVIII   My days have sped away, like, says Job, the threads of a cloth, when a weaver holds burning straw in his hand. Then, if there is any end sticking out, it is suddenly whisked away. And I no longer fear any onslaught, for at death all is assuaged.

In the event, it is not from the parable of the prodigal son in St Luke's Gospel that Villon quotes, but from the Book of Ecclesiastes, using a scholar's trick of giving special meaning to a quotation by isolating it from its context. The contradiction to which Villon alludes is not so sharp if we insert the link that he omitted (his borrowing is italicised): '*Rejoice, o young man, in thy youth*, and let thy heart cheer thee in the days of thy youth, and walk in the ways of thine heart, and in the sight of thine eyes: but know thou that for all these things God will bring thee into judgment. Therefore remove sorrow from thy heart and put away evil from the flesh: for *childhood and youth are vanity*.' (11, 9-10). No matter: to make excuses for his misdemeanours, with whatever degree of irony, by referring to the Bible, was a clever move. In his early years he heeded only the exhortation, ignoring the warning, thereby illustrating, though he did not realise it at the time, the Ecclesiast's ultimate condemnation of youth's frivolity, a condemnation which gives a kind of inevitability to Villon's 'jeunesse folle'. And now the Book of Job, the book of all books for those who must endure present miseries and memories of lost happiness. This time it is paraphrase, not direct quotation: 'My days are swifter than a weaver's shuttle, and are spent without hope' (7, 6). This vivid picture of the weaver ridding his cloth of loose ends by burning them with straw is not, it would seem, a literary reminiscence (at least none has so far been found) but a picture in Villon's mind of something he had seen done, a reminder for us that in his text the scholar's world meets the real world. His verse amalgamates both, in a blend that is Villon's alone. The last two lines (223-24) introduce a new note, the first hint of a theme soon to swell to a climax and that will produce the finest of all Villon's lyric verse: death ends everything.

XXIX   Where are the pleasant companions whom I frequented in bygone days, who sang and spoke so well, so pleasing in deed and word? Some are dead and stiff, nothing remains of them now. May they have rest in paradise, and may God save those remaining.

XXX   And others have become, thanks be to God, great lords and masters. Others beg quite naked and see bread only in the windows. Others have entered the cloisters of Celestine and Carthusian monks, booted and gaitered like oyster-fishers. There you see their varying fortunes.

XXXI   To the great masters may God grant that they act righteously, living in peace and quiet. There is nothing to change in their lot, and it is good to say nothing further about them. But to the poor who, like me, have no resources, God grant patience. The others lack nothing, for they have ample bread and pittance.

XXXII   They have good wines, often drawn from the wood, sauces, broths, large fish, tarts, flans, eggs fried, poached, scrambled, done in all sorts of ways. They are not like stone-masons, whom it is such hard labour to serve. They need no butlers, each takes pains to pour out for himself.

A most important change is heralded by stanza XXIX. The 'je' that for long has been paramount now takes second place, moving to one side as Villon parades before us a long train of companions of his youth. The literary 'persona' will step to the front of the stage again from time to time, but for shorter periods, and the limelight will fall increasingly on others who embody, in differing ways, some aspect or other of his life, as though he comes gradually to the discovery that he can best express his own feelings by evoking the experiences and sufferings of others. Nostalgia seems to penetrate the very sounds of the line, not only in stanza XXIX, the first that both begins and ends its rhymes with nasal vowels (*galans:parlans — maintenant:remanant*; the next one so to do is LVI, another nostalgia-charged stanza, evoking 'le bon temps'); there are also numbers in the interior of the lines, their muted sounds evoking the melancholy of happier times lost forever. The pace, too, is slowed down by the accentual pattern in stanza XXIX (a very strongly marked 4 + 4 in the third line, a weaker 3 + 5 in the fourth). Villon's first thought is for those of his companions who are dead. The wording, as usual, is blunt and direct. 'Mort', like its English counterpart, is frequently replaced by a euphemism, especially in verse, such as 'trespassé' or 'disparu', or 'qui n'est plus'; here, not only is it given direct expression, it is also reinforced: 'mors *et roidiz*'. There is no softening of the tragedy, no veil of gently alluding terms to avoid shocking the reader.

The rich, the poor, the religious orders — stanzas XXX and XXXI present them in the same order. Strangely, no trace of envy is shown of the first category, which receives two matter-of-fact lines in stanza XXX and four in stanza XXXI. The poor receive the same amount of attention in each stanza: two lines only. The ill-clad beggars who see bread only in the shop-windows is one of Villon's most vivid portrayals (see below, p.97). He fastens unerringly on the detail that counts, the short, pithy expression that strikes to the very heart of reality. The monks occupy the latter half of stanza XXX and the last two lines only of XXXI which serve as an introduction to the whole of XXXII. But what is this about being booted and gaitered like oyster-fishers? The religious orders are frequently satirised in the literature of the period because of their wealth and the gulf between what they preached and what they practised, but a more grotesque image was never applied to them than this one. But there is more point to the simile than that. The monks are supposed to be discalceate, or at any rate to be wearing only the simplest of sandals in accordance with their vows of poverty. Villon is really saying that they have departed so far from these vows that it is as though they are wearing boots up to their thighs: they live in comfort and luxury, just as their simple 'bread and pittance' ('pittance' means literally food given out of charity) in fact consists of all these delectable items listed in stanza XXXII. Such an abundance, and such ease in pouring out their own drinks, awaken Villon's envy, and suggest that he himself has not known such conditions for a long time, if ever. It is at least certain that he had lived on a meagre diet in the prison from which he was newly released. The reference to the stone-masons and their hard-working labourers is yet another of Villon's vignettes, surely coming from something he has observed for himself.

XXXIII I have become involved in this digression, which does not serve my case in any way. I am no judge, no clerk to punish or absolve misdeeds. I am the most imperfect of all men, praised be the gentle Jesus Christ! Let them obtain their satisfaction through me! But what I have written is written.

XXXIV Let us leave the Church where it is and speak about something more agreeable. This subject matter does not please everybody, it is tiresome and unpleasant. Poverty, downcast and grieving, always spiteful and rebellious, makes a cutting remark. If it dares not make it, it thinks it.

The avowal at the beginning of stanza XXXIII that his pen has run away with him, carrying him along paths he had not intended to take, suggests that he is writing with a well defined motivation — self-justification — but without a clear overall plan. This declaration of his own unworthiness to pronounce sentence on others for their misdeeds is followed by a brief, half-hearted and wholly unconvincing gesture of apology quickly cancelled out by the last line with its parody of Pontius Pilate's reply to the Jews: 'What I have written I have written' (John, 19, 22). The solid fare enjoyed by the monks serves to throw harsh light on the deprivation of the poor 'comme moy'. Hence the way is open to develop the theme of poverty, and, in so doing, to revert once more to his own plight. Stanza XXXIV is still couched in general terms; its first line was a proverbial expression which came to mean, significantly enough 'we have to accept the inevitable'. Although it is only in the sixteenth century that it is firmly attested with this extended meaning, it is clearly in this tone that Villon uses it here, capturing both the haplessness and bitterness of poverty. Stanza XXXIV concludes with another of Villon's pithy remarks (cf. XXV, XXVIII, XXXII, XXXIII, etc.), itself a 'parole cuisante' emphasising the resentment felt by the poor and downtrodden, particularly towards the well-to-do religious orders, a reminder also that the poor do not and cannot acquiesce in the social conditions which condemn them to their misery. It is far from being a picture of stoic acceptance that Villon gives us (Robert Louis Stevenson accused him of writing 'a calumny on the noble army of the poor'!, see *49*, p.165).

XXXV   I have been poor since my youth, of poor and humble origin. My father never possessed great wealth, nor did his grandfather, called Horace. Poverty follows and trails us all. On the tombs of my ancestors, whose souls may God embrace, no crowns and no sceptres are to be seen.

XXXVI   When I'm moaning about my poverty, often my heart says to me: "Man, do not grieve so much, and don't moan so much if you have not as much as had Jacques Cœur. Better to be alive beneath coarse common cloth poor, than to have been a lord, and to be rotting beneath a fine tombstone!"

'Born to poverty, condemned to poverty, I never stood a chance.' This renewed note of self-justification, not exempt from self-pity, hardly tallies with the earlier confession (stanza XXVI) that the way to a comfortable, house-owning existence had been open to him, and he had not taken it. It is all too easy to point to contradictions in Villon's self-analysis, but this apparent weakness is in reality a strength, adding to the impression that the literary 'persona' is a creature of flesh and blood. Surely, this *is* the real Villon — who can resist this illusion? — quite unable, as most of us are, to see himself in any very clear perspective, unable to determine the exact degree of responsibility that he himself had to accept for his condition, clear only on one thing: that he was at the most only partly to blame — apart from that, able to argue the case one way or the other according to the mood and the moment. In his conflicting attitudes towards himself, Villon is a kind of Montaigne *avant la lettre*. The literary 'persona' is transformed into the common man only too well aware of his mortality. Villon would surely have been happy to echo Montaigne's 'Je suis moi-même la forme entière de l'humaine condition', though he might well have added some wry and contradictory qualification such as 'mais surtout du plus bas estat'.

In stanza XIV Villon had written: 'Je suis pecheur ...' but now he writes, not 'Je suis povre ...' but 'Povre je suis ...' deliberately throwing the adjective into relief, making it a sort of *leitmotiv*: 'povre ... povre ... povreté' in stanza XXXV, 'povreté ... povre' in stanza XXXVI. On this last occurrence the adjective stands out even more starkly since it is used as a 'rejet' ('overflow') with a strong sense pause immediately following it. And what are we to make of the reference to his great-grandfather 'nommé Orrace'? Whether this is factual or not is not known, but there is a distinct possibility that the name is flung in whimsically to suit the rhyme, the implication being that his forebear was any Tom, Dick or Harry, a commoner of low degree. The negative image of the last three lines of stanza XXXV vividly represents the absence of all status and wealth that had characterised the family throughout its history. Stanza XXXVI, from lamentation on his poverty, leads in its second line to self-

consolation, hence to a dialogue with himself: such conver-
sational patterns, with the direct speech which they involve,
contribute frequently to the impact Villon's *Testament* makes on
the reader (see above, p.18). Jacques Cœur was the richest
roturier in the France of Villon's day, whose splendid town-
house can still be seen in Bourges. He had died five years before
Villon wrote the *Testament*. The rich man's tombstone ends this
stanza also, but very differently: to possess it is, after all, no
more to be envied than to be without it is to be lamented, if the
choice is between having been rich and being dead, or being poor
but still alive. In the last resort, the human condition has no
favourites.

> XXXVII   Than to have been a lord! ... What are you
> saying? Lord, alas! is he that no more? According to the
> psalms of David, he shall no longer recognise his place.
> And as for the rest, I put it away from me. It does not
> belong to me, a sinner. I leave it to the theologians, for
> that is the duty of a preacher.

> XXXVIII   And I am not, think on it well, the son of an
> angel wearing a diadem with a star or other orb. My father
> is dead, God have his soul! As for the body, it lies beneath
> the slab. I realise my mother will die. She knows it well, the
> poor woman, and the son will not tarry long.

Self-consolation leads to self-questioning. What could sound
more natural, more convincing, than the first two lines of stanza
XXXVII, repeating as a question, or exclamation, part of what
has just been said, and querying it in the spirit of 'surely that
cannot be?' It is almost an irritation to learn that this was a trick
of style, known as *ratiocinatio*, taught and practised by medieval
rhetoricians. No poet has ever made a highly developed acquired
technique seem more natural. The lines following are probably a
reference to that highly apposite, and beautiful, passage from
Psalm 103: 'As for man, his days are as grass: as a flower of the
field, so he flourisheth. For the wind passeth over it, and it is
gone; and the place thereof shall know it no more' (verses

15-16).[7] As in stanza XXXIII, Villon denies that he has any right to make pronouncements on others, the 'seurplus' being the fate of human beings after their death. The name Jacques Cœur has launched Villon on a digression just as did the name Thibault d'Aussigny in the opening stanza, though in a radically different vein. In stanza XXXVIII he returns yet again to his basic theme: himself, linked to the thoughts newly rising in his mind on the omnipotence of death. He too has nothing immortal about him, he is no son of an angel wearing a diadem, symbol of eternity and perhaps seen by Villon in stained glass windows or mural paintings. The reference to his parents which takes up more than half of this stanza, has a strong ring of authenticity, and adds to the picture that Villon is building up of himself in opposition to authority's view of him as a wastrel and a criminal.

XXXIX   I know that poor men and rich men, wise men and fools, priests and laymen, nobles, villains, the generous and the mean, small and tall, handsome and ugly, ladies with high-turned collars, of whatever estate in life, wearing the hair style of the aristocracy or bourgeoisie, Death seizes without exception.

XL   And whether it is Paris or Helen dying, whoever dies, dies in pain such that he loses wind and breath. His gall bursts over his heart, then he sweats, God knows what sweat! And there is no-one to relieve him of his pains, for he has no child, no brother or sister, who would then stand pledge for him.

XLI   Death makes him tremble, grow pale, his nose curve, his veins stretch, his neck swell out, his flesh grow soft, his joints and sinews grow and distend. Woman's body, you so tender, smooth, gentle, so precious, must you await these ills? Yes, or go living to the heavens.

---

[7] One MS has the reading 'congnoistras', continuing the second person singular of the preceding lines. This is possible, and could be a reference to Psalm 37, 10: 'For yet a little while, and the wicked shall not be: yea, thou shalt diligently consider his place, and it shall not be'. The Rychner-Henry edition prefers 'congnoistra', *20*B, p.45.

At this stage the literary 'persona' does not remain the subject for long. The 'je' that begins stanza XXXIX is no longer the centre of attention, merely an agent for the expression of a universal truth. So now the pendulum swings back, and death the leveller holds the scene as a flow of people pass before our eyes in groups strongly contrasted, yet all based on common 'everybody' formulae, and united in their grim and inevitable fate, culminating in ladies of different social levels, forerunners in a minor key of a theme soon to be expressed in a major one, in the first ballade of the *Testament*. (Like the other ballades in the *Testament*, this one has no title in the MSS. The titles *Ballade des dames (seigneurs) du temps jadis, Ballade en vieil langage françoys* etc. were provided by Clément Marot, in his sixteenth-century edition of Villon's poetry, arguably the first 'critical' edition of the works of any French poet.) So often a theme receives an early, and brief, mention, soon to be given fuller treatment, as though we witness its first occurring in Villon's mind, then its development from an embryo to full expression. The ladies with high collars to their dresses belonged to the nobility, characterised also by the 'atour' hair style, reaching high over their heads in the 'hennin', whereas those wearing the less spectacular 'bourreletz' belonged to the bourgeoisie.

Remarkable in stanza XXXI is the grammatical structure. It would have been more usual to begin with what is here the last line, so giving the stereotyped word order subject-verb-object, but how much more dramatic is the sentence in the form chosen by Villon. What appears to be a protracted subject suddenly, unexpectedly, is transformed into direct object. The reader is likely to anticipate a line such as 'Meurent tous sans excepcion'. Villon's wording has a far greater impact, with the personification *Mort* dominating them all, the harshness of the verb *saisit* driving the point ruthlessly home. The list is not allowed to lose impact through being too general; after seven contrasting pairs, he picks out precise details which maintain close contact with living reality and which from their very nature hint at the vanity of human existence. As in similar vignettes elsewhere in the *Testament* the subject is the opposite sex (cf. stanzas LVI and CXLV, and contrast what is said below (p.58) about the

jester and the old harlot). A change of orchestration in stanza
XL, for the theme is not to be death after all but the act of
dying, and it is the verb, repeated three times in two lines, which
provides the *leitmotiv*. The anatomical details of the following
lines reflect ancient Greek beliefs about what happened to the
dying; similar references are found in other fifteenth-century
works and are owed to a long tradition doubtless preserved in
the universities (see *20*B, pp.49-51). Again a change of
orchestration, the point of view quickly passing from that of the
person dying to that of the one looking on with horror at this
prefiguration of his own last moments on earth. It is not Villon's
way to pass over, or even tone down, the distressing details, but
on the other hand he does not dwell on them in an unnecessarily
lurid fashion, or make them the starting-point, as so many of his
contemporaries would have done, of some lengthy, moralising
homily. This shudder of dread ends in a dramatic and
unheralded fashion. In a later torment, facing the miseries of old
age, Villon turns, as here, to women for consolation. Let no
wearisome Freudian interpretation be invoked: Villon finds here
the epitome of human beauty, death's greatest triumph, therefore, and the human tragedy at its most acute. As the irony of
the last line clearly implies, only the Virgin Mary was able to go
living to the heavens.

Ballade of Ladies of bygone days

Tell me where, in what land, is Flora, the beauty of Rome,
Archipiades or Thaïs so much like her, Echo speaking
when a noise is made over river or lake, whose beauty was
more than human. But where are last year's snows?

Where is the very wise Heloïse, for whom Peter Abelard at
Saint Denis was castrated and made a monk? For his love
he suffered this torment. Similarly, where is the queen who
ordered Buridan to be thrown into the Seine in a sack? But
where are last year's snows?

Queen Blanche, white as a lily, who sang with a siren's
voice, Bertha Flatfoot, Beatrice, Alice, Arambourg who

held the Maine, and Joan the brave maid of Lorraine
whom the English burned at Rouen. Where are they,
where, sovereign Virgin? But where are last year's snows?

Prince, do not ask this week, or this year, where they have
gone, lest I bring you back to this refrain: But where are
last year's snows?

It is important to note that this ballade, the structure of
which, as regards number of stanzas, lines and the rhyme-
scheme, is entirely conventional, is very closely related to the
stanzas which precede it. The seeds of the ballade are in the 'ubi
sunt?' (= 'where are they?') theme, conventional enough in the
Middle Ages, first adumbrated in the fate of Jacques Cœur,
then Paris and Helen of Troy, those lovers whose ghosts hover
over the entire ballade, their names providing the haunting
rhymes in *-is* and *-aine* on which each of the three stanzas is
principally based. We have seen that the *Testament* does not
involve a simple juxtaposition of themes, one following the
other in mechanical fashion or in a neat and rational progression. From the very beginning of the work, one theme is
enmeshed in another, and it could be argued that there is a kind
of emotional logic in that one feeling leads naturally, inevitably,
to the next one. The emotional chain is continuous and
unbroken. Even this ballade does not freeze the movement, the
mood in the envoi being very different from that at the
beginning. The unavoidable impression is that Villon *lives* his
poetry. It is not static, but evolves as his feelings evolve, written
very likely over a short period of time, and, so far at least, in one
continuous surge.

Marot's title is treacherous, for it can so easily lead to an
excessively sentimental interpretation of this most famous of all
French ballades. The first stanza is a sublimation, a drifting-
away on the wings of reverie from the fetid physical horrors of
the preceding stanzas. The first figures to be named loom up
vaguely from the mists of time. It is enough to note that modern
commentators are embarrassed by the fact that there was more
than one Flora in antiquity, more than one Thaïs. These are little

more than names from the dim and distant past floating in Villon's mind. As for Archipiades, a name whose very sounds and strangeness inevitably give it a romantic aura, it was in fact a corruption of Alcibiades, an Athenian general, a reference to whose handsome appearance misled, not merely François Villon, but almost the entire Middle Ages. As far as Villon and his contemporaries were concerned, Archipiades was the name of a beautiful woman of the remote past, and it is doubtful that he could have added any supplementary information at all — just the shadow of a name, and a poet's imagination (not a faculty, admittedly, that Villon indulges a great deal). And what could be more ethereal or wraith-like than the nymph Echo, heard over river and lake (a literary reminiscence going back to Ovid's *Metamorphoses*, though Villon may have encountered it in the works of more recent poets, such as Guillaume de Lorris, author of the first half of the thirteenth-century *Roman de la Rose*) who concludes the first group of this ghostly cortège of the 'snows of yester-year' to use Rossetti's famous translation, very apt since 'antan' in Villon's day meant not so much 'bygone days' as 'the previous year'? Villon's metaphor is an extremely beautiful one (all the more so when contrasted with the gruesome details of the preceding stanzas), and original. Scholars have attempted to find earlier instances of it elsewhere, but without success apart from one diligent researcher who found something similar in Hungarian (see *48* and *38*)!

In the second stanza it immediately becomes apparent that there is a change of mood, as occurs throughout the *Testament*, reading from one stanza to the next. Heloïse is much closer to Villon's age in time, and immediately, and very clearly, recognisable to his contemporaries, and to us. It is rather like a blurred image on a screen being brought suddenly into clear focus. Well known was the story of the tragic twelfth-century lovers, whose letters had been translated from Latin into French by Jean de Meun. Equally well known, at least in Paris in the 1460s, was the legend telling that Jeanne de Navarre, wife of Philippe le Bel (King of France from 1285 to 1314) had had a series of lovers whom — after a brief affair — she had cast into the Seine from her bedroom window, amongst them Buridan,

professor at the University, who had arranged for a barge full of
hay to pass beneath the palace windows at the crucial moment,
so that his end was not the nasty one suggested by Villon's
poem. This mischievous and, unhappily perhaps, unfounded
tale may have originated in the scurrilous behaviour, not of
Philippe's wife, but of his two daughters-in-law, who were put
to death along with their lovers. So well known was the legend
that Villon had no need to name the queen. But why does he
choose these two heroines, and what does he tell us about them?
Precious little could well be the answer to this last question, for
only two of the eight lines concern them, the rest being taken up
with the unhappy fate of their lovers, on which Villon insists at
the risk of losing his central theme. Even remembering that
Villon did not give this poem the title *Ballade des dames* ... or
any title at all, one cannot dismiss the impression that this most
digression-prone of poets is here teetering on the brink of yet
another of his lengthy asides. This stanza in fact provides the
first fleeting hint (as we have noted so many others) of a theme
soon to be carried to a climax in its turn: that love makes fools
of all men. Abelard and Buridan are merely the forerunners of
quite a series, including Solomon, Samson, Orpheus, Narcissus,
David and St John the Baptist, and, trailing behind, no less a
figure than François Villon himself, who finds consolation of a
kind in treating the entire world as a sort of projection of his
own woes. But surely this sour note is out of place in this
context? Some ladies! Some snow! We must not over-sentiment-
alize, as did the pre-Raphaelites, the poem's beauty, nor must
we look on Villon's attitude to love as necessarily sour or even in
any way critical. It is Villon's deep conviction — and indeed that
of the entire age — that love brings disaster to all men; this is
eventually to inspire the thoroughly scurrilous and amusing
poem referred to above, but no criticism of women is intended:
he writes, as he declares, 'Sans l'honneur des dames blasmer'
(stanza LXIII). It is simply human nature that makes things the
way they are ('feminine nature' is Villon's expression), and he
sees love and all its consequences as much a part of life as is the
certain knowledge that we must all face death. Heloïse and
Queen Jeanne de Navarre were remarkable for having ensnared

two very eminent men; Abelard is therefore a measure of Heloïse's greatness as Buridan is of the queen's.

Beauty is the theme of the first stanza ('la *belle* Romaine ...', 'Qui *beaulté* ot ...'), love is the theme of the second, heroism that of the third. The veils of mystery, briefly lifted in the poem's central stanza, fall once again in the third. Even Villon's contemporaries may have had difficulty in identifying some of these figures. 'La reine blanche' meant 'dowager queen' but neither history nor legend has preserved the name of any such queen renowned for her beautiful voice. Is the reference to Blanche de Castille, mother of King Louis IX (who became Saint Louis)? She survived her husband by a number of years, so that there were two reasons for calling her 'Blanche', which may be why Villon adds 'comme liz' — none whiter than she. She was of tremendous help to her son who succeeded to the throne at the age of twelve. Berthe au plat pié (see *20*B, p.55), Bietrix, Aliz are mythical figures drawn from medieval French epic works. Villon's precise source, for long unknown, has only recently been identified. The very sound of the names was clearly a factor: Haramburgis, the Latin form of Erembourg (countess of Anjou and Maine who died in 1126), is one of six in the poem with the euphonic ending -*is*. After five shadowy figures from long ago, we are brought sharply from myth to reality, and into Villon's own times, with Joan of Arc, then to the Virgin Mary, greatest figure of them all, universally revered in Villon's day, familiar to all through the teachings of the Church and in statues and stained-glass windows. The effect is to give an extraordinary depth and perspective to the stanza, the later figures sharply outlined, the earlier ones little more than shapes in the darkness, as though we look back down the long tunnel of history into a twilight background.

The envoi was by Villon's day a traditional, and optional, feature of the ballade. Originally, this concluding half-stanza was addressed to the 'Prince du puy', the 'puy' being a poetry festival or competition held in several towns throughout France, the North in particular. The 'Prince' presided over the festival. Later, as in Villon's poem, 'Prince' could refer to no particular person, or no such invocation need be present, as the next two

ballades show. This envoi heralds a change and deserves careful
note. (On the tense involved, see *20*B, p.56.) There is no point in
the rhetorical question of the refrain, for it will never get an
answer: nobody can say what has become of them, there is no
solution to the problem.

A sort of kinetic energy inspires this ballade. It moves along,
changing from one stanza to the next exactly as does the rest of
the *Testament*. A title such as Marot's implies a single basic
theme, and it may be for this very reason that Villon himself
provided no title at all, beyond, possibly (judging from the
manuscripts) the one used: Ballade, which concerns form alone,
not theme. The very refrain undergoes quite dramatic change
and so has little unifying effect, the 'snows of yester-year'
applying first to those beautiful women of long ago — its most
appropriate application, surely — then those inspirers of great
passion, then the heroic women of past and present, finally
being degraded to a vain rhetorical question which we are urged
to discard. It remains, however, that the image is a very beautiful one. The poem epitomises Villon's lyricism in that it is a rich
panoply of emotions in which we may all find differing shades
and moods. It is a kaleidoscope, every shake of which can reveal
new patterns (see *34*, and *31*, Ch. II).

Ballade of Lords of bygone days

Moreover, where is Calixtus the third, latest of that name
to die, who held the papacy for four years? Alphonso,
King of Aragon, the gracious Duke of Bourbon, and
Arthur Duke of Brittany, and the brave Charles VII? But
where is the noble Charlemagne?

Similarly, the Scottish King, half of whose face, it is said,
was as purple as an amethyst from his forehead right down
to his chin? The renowned King of Cyprus, alas! and the
brave King of Spain, whose name I do not know? But
where is the noble Charlemagne?

I give up saying anything more; the world is but deception.
No-one can resist death or find any provision against it. I

ask one further question: Lancelot King of Bohemia where
has he got to? Where's his grand-dad? But where is the
noble Charlemagne?

Where is Clacquin, the brave Breton? Where the Count
Dauphin of Auvergne, and the brave late Duke of
Alençon? But where is the noble Charlemagne?

Marot's title for this second ballade is even less appropriate than
the one he inflicted on its predecessor, since most of the figures
mentioned here are from quite recent times. The beginning
'Moreover' makes it quite clear that this is meant to be read in
conjunction with the preceding poem, so that it cannot be
isolated as an anthology piece or copied in a manuscript apart
from Villon's other works, a device he uses again in the third
and final ballade of this series, with the opening line: 'For
whether it be ...' It is, of course, possible to isolate the first of
the series, and this has been very frequently done from the
fifteenth to the twentieth centuries inclusive, much to the detri-
ment of the poem, part of whose effect lies in its complex
relationship with its context. The first stanza of this second
poem gathers momentum as it proceeds: after devoting three
lines to the Pope, it is a matter of a mere list, one line, one name,
rather like a film that is speeded up. It would be contrary to the
very spirit of the poem, and pointless, to devote much time to
identifying these individuals. Alphonso I, King of Aragon,
Arthur III, Duke of Brittany, had both died, like Pope Calixtus
III, in 1458, Charles I, Duke of Bourbon, in 1456, whereas
Charles VII had died only a few months before Villon was
writing, in July, 1461. The refrain falls flat in comparison with
the preceding one, substituting a name, illustrious though it may
be, for the poetically beautiful metaphor. Villon's flights of
poetic fancy owe little to the male of the species, unless it be
himself; we shall have a good illustration of this before long (in
the contrast between stanzas XLII-XLV on the one hand, and
XLVI-LVI on the other). The Scottish King with the large birth-
mark on his face — what an odd, indeed grotesque, reason for
his inclusion here! — was James II, who died in 1460. The
unnamed King of Cyprus was probably John III who died in

1458, but it is a disservice to the poem to provide the name, since Villon flaunts his inability to produce it, or rather, his indifference. A mood of impatience and flippancy is developing rapidly: what does it all matter anyway, we are not going to get anywhere. The stanza carries this mood further forward: it's utterly hopeless to protest against death — the subject triggered off, it will be remembered, by the mention in stanza XXXVI of Jacques Cœur. Lancellot, King of Bohemia (died 1457) — Villon really means Ladislas, but the confusion of the name with that of the more familiar one of the Arthurian hero (an example of 'popular etymology') was common enough — brings this stanza to a climax which grotesquely parodies its counterpart in the corresponding stanza of the preceding ballade; 'tayon' meant a young sapling retained through three successive thinnings of a forest, and hence was used as a child's word for the third generation. The envoi fires off in rapid succession a further three names over which it would be otiose to dwell: Clacquin, the nickname of the famous Bertrand du Guesclin, scourge of the English, who died in 1380; the Dauphin of Auvergne, probably Berand II, who died in 1400; and the Duke of Alençon was John I who died at Agincourt in 1415. It has been pointed out that there is a pattern of a kind in this ballade: more important than the year of their death was the age at which each died. The first stanza groups together older men, the second men of early middle age, the third younger men, the order being repeated in the first three lines of the envoi, so it is as though the most striking examples are reserved for the end, a sort of progression towards what a later age has called the 'absurd': 'Ladislas' (Laszlo V) was only eighteen when he died (see *20*B, pp.58-59). The poem ironically equates, in its third stanza, the tragic and the futile. 'A quoi bon', the shrug of the shoulders that ends the preceding ballade, is now the all-pervading tone.

Ballade in Old French

For whether it be the holy pope, wearing the surplice and with the amice on his head, who girds on nothing but holy stoles, with which he takes the devil, all hot with rage, by the neck, he dies as well as the lay brothers, snatched away from this life, the wind carries away as much.

Indeed, or whether it be the golden-fisted emperor of Constantinople, or the very noble King of France, distinguished above all other Kings, who for the worship of the mighty God built churches and convents, if in his time he was honoured, the wind carries away as much.

Or whether it be the noble, the wise Dauphin of Vienne and Grenoble, or the eldest son of the lord of Dijon, Salins and Dôle, or as many of their private household, heralds, trumpeters, men-at-arms, have they eaten and drunk their fill? The wind carries away as much.

Princes are destined to die, and everyone else who is alive. Even if they are angered or vexed by this, the wind carries away as much.

And so Villon, in a parody of his looking to the past, has decided to write this last ballade of the series in Old French! Not too successfully either, though it could be that the copyists have let him down on occasions — they were probably even more ignorant of archaic spellings and forms than he was. No names are quoted now, only titles of the high and mighty, the futility of the protest having been amply demonstrated at the level of the named individual: the Pope begins the cortège, with a quick side-glance at the lay brothers, the Emperor of Constantinople and the King of France sharing the second section, the son of the King and of the Duke of Burgundy the third, with members of their household putting in an appearance at the rear: a progressive moving-down the scale of titles, from highest to lowest, it makes no difference, for all must pass into oblivion. (Stanzas CLXII-CLXIII return to this same theme, differently presented.) Have they, asks Villon irreverently, 'shoved beneath their noses', we could translate in spirit, 'crammed their cake-holes full', that is to say, had a good old fling while they could. This faster-moving, scurrilous ballade brings the series to a triumphant and uproarious climax, contrasting utterly with the mood with which these three ballades began: *might as well make a laugh out of it*, Villon concludes, *because there is absolutely nothing else we can do*.

Some details of this ballade need elucidation, although what really matters is the spirit in which it is written. The reference to the Pope's wearing the amice on his head seems odd, but this square of white linen, now worn on the shoulders, was indeed worn on the head in the Middle Ages. The first stanza refers to exorcism; the priest's weapon against the devil was, not a sword, but his stole. 'Ly mauffez', according to the conventions of Old French, should have been 'le mauffé', and even the exigencies of rhyme did not allow the one to be substituted for the other: there is no point in our being pedantic about the matter, but the former was in fact nominative only, the latter accusative. The gold-fisted emperor refers to depictions Villon had seen of the emperor bearing in his hand a golden sphere, symbol of imperial power, while the references to the King of France who built churches and convents seems specific — one thinks of Louis IX, Saint Louis, that is — but is unlikely to be so in view of the tonality of the poem: all French Kings distinguished themselves in this manner is the point. The old title Dauphin de Viennois had been shortened to Dauphin and reserved for the King's eldest son since the Dauphiné had been joined to the royal household in 1349, while the title of the son of the 'lord of Dijon, Salins and Dôle', i.e. of the duke of Burgundy, was the comte de Charollais. The envoi reflects old conventions in its first word but a statement about the princes replaces the direct address to them (or to him as was more often the case). Both poem and series end on a note of anti-climax, for the mood of protest, this revolt against death, has quite worked itself out. All Villon's moods pass quickly away, none occupying more than a few stanzas.

In the next stanza, back we come to the prime motivating force of the *Testament*: Villon himself:

XLII   Since popes, Kings, sons of Kings, even those conceived in the wombs of queens are buried, dead and cold
and their Kingdoms pass to other hands, shall not I, a poor

pedlar of words, die? Yes ... if it please God! As long as I have had my day, a decent death does not displease me.

How remote now that terror of dying, out of which grew the series of three ballades! The paroxysm is followed by a resigned shrug of the shoulders. To remove the ballades from the *Testament* would be to make nonsense of the entire passage. Clearly they are not mere interpolations or decoration. True, they herald a change of mood, but they themselves continue to change. Villon's attitude evolves constantly, not just from one ballade to the next, but even within each one. He has worked his way towards this conclusion. Viewed in the context, it is an entirely natural outcome of his train of thought, or rather, of emotions.

Two expressions give difficulty: 'povre mercerot de regnes' is usually translated as 'poor pedlar of Rennes', but Villon had no connections with that town as far as is known, and the expression is found nowhere else. A recent suggestion is that 'regnes' is an altogether different word deriving from Old French 'araisner', 'to address somebody', meaning therefore, 'speech, discourse, words', appropriate in the context, but still hypothetical (see *20*B, pp.63-64 and *6*, p.361). The second difficulty concerns the expression 'faire ses estraines' (mod. 'étrennes'), also not attested elsewhere. In association with 'mercerot', 'estraines' could mean 'first sale made in the day' (see *20*B, p.64) so perhaps the meaning in this context could be 'provided my writings have had some success'. More generally, 'estraines' can refer to pleasure, hence 'provided I have had my day', i.e. had my fun out of life, which certainly fits the context very well indeed. At least, there can be no doubt about the meaning of 'Honneste mort' in the last line: it excludes execution at the hands of the law, the shadow of which has already fallen across several stanzas and reappears in others of his poems. Fear of the death pangs, that gripped him so violently, has now vanished utterly, as though Villon has exorcised it with his ballades.

XLIII   This world is not everlasting, whatever the rich

plunderer may think. We are all beneath the sword of death. Take this comfort, poor old man, who, when young, had the reputation of being an amusing jester, who would be held for a fool and a knave if, in old age, he began to jest.

XLIV   Now he has to beg, for necessity forces him to do so. He longs today as yesterday for his death, sadness weighs down so heavily on his heart. Often, were it not for his fear of God, he would commit a horrible deed, and it happens that he does infringe God's law in this, and that he does away with himself.

XLV   For if he gave pleasure in his youth, now nothing he says pleases — an old monkey is always disagreeable, no grimace it makes can amuse — if he is silent in order to please others, he is held for a worn-out fool. If he speaks, he is told to shut up and that there is no crop left in his plum-tree.

Here is the second of Villon's three surrogates (after Diomedes of stanza XVII; the third is the Belle Heaulmière, who appears in stanza XLVI and occupies no fewer than fourteen stanzas), the least successful of the three. After the degradation wrought by poverty comes that wrought by death, and now, old age; only with the first of these could Villon remain squarely in the foreground: of poverty he had direct experience, whereas the other tribulations are ahead of him still, although in another work he envisaged his own death in a grim and realistic physical portrayal. For three stanzas Villon tries to interest himself in this pathetic figure of the old clown, without really succeeding; the clown, a thinly drawn, shadowy puppet, is allotted no direct speech whereas the other two surrogates are, rather as though he never caught Villon's ear and attention. Villon sees him, less as an individual, more as a premonition of the fate that awaits him, with his reputation of being, as he says elsewhere, 'ung bon follastre' ('a good jester', stanza CLXXVII). The surrogate clown is soon discarded in favour of the old woman,[8] to whom

[8] If it is true that Villon had been imprisoned by the Bishop of Orleans because

Villon devotes, not a mere 21 lines, but 116, of which no fewer than 104 are spoken by her. She springs into vivid and altogether convincing life. Just as, facing death, Villon's real inspiration and consolation came from woman — the *Ballade des seigneurs* is as sketchy in its way as the portrait of the clown — so now, confronting old age and seeing yet another aspect of the tragedy of the human condition, after a brief glance in the direction of the worn-out old clown — surely a promising subject, as shown by nineteenth-century exploitation of it? — Villon, instinctively it seems, turns to the opposite sex:

XLVI   In the same way these poor old women, who are old and have no resources, when they see the young girls borrowing their services in secret, ask God why they were born so soon, and by what right. Our Lord remains quite silent, for, in an argument with them, he would lose.

XLVII   It seems to me I can hear lamenting the whore who was an armouress, wishing she was a girl and speaking in this manner: "Oh harsh and cruel old age, why have you struck me down so soon? What is there, what, to prevent me from striking myself and killing myself with this blow?

XLVIII   You have taken away from me the high authority that Beauty had granted me over clerks, merchants and men of the church, for then there was no man born who would not have given me his entire possessions — whatever repentance he would have had — provided I had yielded up to him what beggars now refuse.

Before singling out a particular one as his new surrogate, Villon, who not long ago was lamenting over his own destitution (stanza XXIII), paints a sympathetic portrait of the lonely old women driven to giving their services to the young prostitutes. (This is the most likely meaning of the difficult line 448 in stanza

of his association with a group of strolling players (see above p.17), there may be a very different explanation for the comparative non-development of the old jester: it was too close to reality and might have run the risk of reviving accusations which had already brought him enough trouble. No such risk with the Belle Heaulmière.

XLVI, see *20*B, pp.69-70. Judging from the ballade soon to
follow, the service consists of advice on how to make the most of
their sexual relationship, a sort of erotic version of 'carpe
diem'.) Having explored the heights in the first ballade of the
Testament, we are now plunged into the depths, even though the
essential theme is unchanged: it is still a harking-back to the
past, still a lament for what time has demolished, but now all
within the space of a lifetime. Hence the change of mood from
one of nostalgia to one of indignation: 'by what right were we
born so soon?' — it slips so easily into direct speech (no such
passage in the stanzas on the old clown) — and this is precisely
what happens in the next stanza. The allegorical 'Vieillesse' is
apostrophised with rhetorical questions which show, once again,
the influence of Villon's training in rhetoric, but they come so
naturally, with such an appearance of spontaneity, that it is
almost offensive to suggest that a literary technique is involved.
Once more we have a fusion of training and observed behaviour,
as in the figure herself. The scurrilous old woman, full of snide
comments on youth, sex and old age, was a stock literary
character used by Ovid early in the first century A.D., and by
Jean de Meun, drawing inspiration from the Latin satirical poet,
in his thirteenth-century *Roman de la Rose*. The influence of
Jean de Meun on Villon for this character is beyond all dispute
(see *20*B, p.71) and yet the very oddity of the detail: 'La belle qui
fut hëaulmiere' (why 'hëaulmiere' when there are countless
words ending in -*iere* involving much more common professions
than a saleswoman in an armourer's shop?) has the ring of truth
about it. It has been established that a 'Belle Heaulmière' was
spoken of in Paris in 1393, so that at the time Villon was writing
(assuming it is the same person) she would have been very old.
That a figure drawn partly from literature as well as from life
should be made to address an allegorical abstraction is not a
promising formula for a convincing portrayal, yet, such is
Villon's involvement (contrast yet again the stanzas on the old
clown), and such his skill as a writer, that the Belle Heaulmière is
by far the most vivid, loquacious and forceful of the many
characters who crowd his poetry — save for the literary
'persona' himself. Now she looks back to her past as he had

looked to his: where he heard the singing and conversation of happy companions, she saw the attentions and blandishments of countless suitors. But her behaviour in those far-off days had not been reprehensible:

> XLIX   I refused it to many a man, which was not great wisdom on my part, for love of a sly fellow to whom I gave my love very fully. Whomsoever I stinted of my love, upon my soul I loved him truly. Now he only treated me roughly, and loved me for my possessions.

> L   He could not maltreat me or trample me underfoot enough to stop me loving him, and had he dragged me along on my back, then told me to kiss him, I would have forgotten all my troubles. The wretch, steeped in vice, would kiss me ... And much good it has done me! What remains to me now? Shame and sin.

> LI   Now he has been dead for the past thirty years and I remain old, white-haired. When I think — alas! of the good times, what I was, what I have become. When I look at myself quite naked — and I see myself changed so much, poor, dried-up, thin, frail, I am almost driven out of my mind.

She had been constant in her affections, devoted to one man, despite his cruel treatment of her, and had remained so until he had died years ago. She is the first, and principal illustration of an argument soon to follow (stanzas LX-LXII): there is no such thing as an immoral woman. All are decent, and respectable, to begin with. It is life, and human nature, that change all that. Such tolerance and breadth of view at this period dominated by the severe moralising of the Church could come only from one with much experience of life, close though he is, in these passages, to what Jean de Meun had written on the same topic. Suffering, and degradation, are fully understood only by those who have endured them themselves.

> LII   What has become of that smooth forehead, fair hair,

arched eyebrows, widely spaced eyes, that pretty look with which I caught the cleverest of men, that lovely straight nose, neither big nor small, the small, well-shaped ears, dimpled chin, bright, open face, and those lovely crimson lips?

LIII   Those lovely little shoulders, long arms and delicate hands, small breasts, firm hips made for passionate combat, wide loins, that little treasure set on large firm thighs within its tiny garden-plot?

LIV   The forehead wrinkled, the hair turned grey, the eyebrows fallen, the eyes dull whose looks and laughter used to catch many a hapless victim, the nose bent, far removed from beauty, ears drooping and heavy, face pale, dead and expressionless, chin roughened, lips flabby.

LV   This is what becomes of human beauty — the arms short, the hands twisted, the shoulders all hunched, breasts, why ask? all withered, the hips just like the tits, as for the little treasure, well! As for the thighs, they are thighs no more, but thighlets, wrinkled like sausages.

LVI   So we look back to the good old times, amongst ourselves, poor stupid old women, squatting low on our haunches, all in a heap like balls of wool, around our tiny fire of hemp-sticks quickly lit, quickly put out... And once we were so lovely! So it happens with many, men and women alike.

It has often been remarked that the psychology is unconvincing in this passage. This is not what it is supposed to be, for the eyes that catalogue in such careful detail the physical charms of the young woman, and the cruel changes wrought by age, are those of *another*, and of a man rather than a woman: it is all purely *external*, purely *visual*, whereas in reality old people complain far more bitterly about their aches and pains and limitation of movement, which torment them far more than their changed appearance. Besides, the inference in stanza LI is that the Belle Heaulmière is looking directly at her body, but we have to do her — or rather the poet — the courtesy of providing a mirror, for what does she see? Forehead, eyebrows, eyes, ears, even her back! It is indeed another who is gazing at this body, not without sexual excitement, moreover, when it is young and attractive,[9] but with all desire extinguished when it is old and repulsive. That other is, of course, François Villon, whose lament over human destiny has abandoned its broad, historical perspectives and reverted to the harsh physical realities depicted in stanzas XL and XLI. It is at the level of life as the individual experiences it that Villon's poetry achieves its most original, and powerful, effects. It is at this level that he pitches the lesson in the concluding picture of the old women squatting around their tiny fire which, like them, is quickly lit, quickly put out, so symbolising their whole existence, *our* whole existence.

'C'est d'umaine beaulté l'yssue' — like the refrain of the first ballade in the *Testament*, this line can lead only to shoulder-shrugging resignation, for nobody can do anything about it. What has brought Villon to write in this vein? If we follow the emotional chain back to the stanzas preceding the three ballades, we find that it begins as a kind of consolation that Villon, alone and destitute, offers himself and others in similar circumstances: even the richest and mightiest of men cannot escape death. Uneven though the social pattern may be, in the end it matters not one jot nor tittle: *you cannot buy your way out of the human condition*. This simple observation could serve as the basis of quite a number of differing attitudes. It could, for example, support an argument in favour of a levelling of the different social strata, but Villon, more lyric poet than moralist or philosopher, goes no further than the 'carpe diem' theme that poets down the ages have sung. It is a roystering, scurrilous version of it that we now have in the old harlot's advice to the young and active practitioners of her trade:

Now bear it in mind, fair glover, so far just a novice [see *20*B, p.79], and you Blanche the slipper-girl, now it's time

---

[9] The portrait is frank but not offensive, the terminology being more delicate than is sometimes realised. 'Sadinet', sexual in the context, is not itself a sexual term. It is still in some French dictionaries as an archaic adjective meaning 'petit et agréable', and is therefore a euphemism in this particular passage.

to know your trade. Take to the right and take to the left,
spare no man I beg you, for old women have no value and
no standing, any more than coins that are out of date.

And you, pretty sausage-girl who are deft at dancing,
Guillemete the tapestry-girl, don't treat your master
scurvily. You'll soon have to put up the shutters. When
you become old and withered, you'll serve nobody any
longer — except an old priest — any more than coins that
are out of date.

Jehanneton the cloak-girl, mind your lover doesn't restrain
your freedom, and Katherine the purse-girl, don't send
men packing, for she who isn't beautiful mustn't show
them ill-grace, but must smile at them. Ugly old age
doesn't solicit love, any more than coins that are out of
date.

Girls, be so good as to take it on yourselves to listen why I
weep and wail: because I cannot put myself in circulation,
any more than coins that are out of date.''

A lively poem in sparkling bad taste, Villon at his mocking best.
The resounding feminine rhymes find a gay lilting echo within
the lines, and the whole sound structure harmonises wonderfully
with the Belle Heaulmière's scandalous admonitions:

Prenez a d*estre* et a sen*estre* ...

Ne mespr*enez* vers vos*tre* mais*tre*
Tost vous fauldra clor*re* fenes*tre*
Quant deviendrez viel*le*, flestr*ie*...

Equally wicked is the wit of remarks such as 'you'll serve
nobody any longer, except an old priest ...'. The lesson, then, is
simple: what is quite certain is that life will mock you in the end,
then cast you aside, so make your protest, however futile, cock a
snook at life, then grab all you can while you can.

LVII   This lesson was given them by the one who in

bygone days was good and beautiful. Well spoken or badly, whatever it's worth, I have had it taken down by my clerk, the scatterbrained Fremin, just as sober as I believe myself to be. If he lets me down, I curse him: it is the clerk who gives the measure of his master.

LVIII   And I perceive the great danger confronting a man in love. And should anyone wish to reproach me with these words, saying: "Listen! If the deceit of those you have named turns you aside from love and repels you, you are acting according to a very foolish fear, for these are women of ill repute.

LIX   If they love only for money, they are only loved for a short time. Freely they love all men, and they laugh when the purse weeps. There is no man who does not run from these women. A decent man, so help me God, spends his time with women of honour and good reputation, with others, no."

At the end of this particular development Villon pauses to reflect on the boldness of what he has just written, and realises that it may be found offensive in some quarters. Far from going back on his words, he sticks to them as on other outspoken occasions (e.g. stanza XXXIII) but he allows himself a flippant and ironical standing-back from his lines: 'she said it, not me, and in any case, my clerk took it down, he's responsible, not me ...' Whether a real person or not (see 6, pp.441-42), Fremin serves above all as a sort of surrogate-scapegoat. In stanza LVIII Villon starts to move more confidently along the track cautiously opened up in the preceding stanza: how to meet objections to what he has just written, since merely to raise a laugh is not enough. His favourite procedure at such moments is to invent an interlocutor who objects to what he has written (cf. stanza III) so that Villon can object to the objection — a clear indication, as pointed out above, that he is measuring keenly the likely effect of his poetry on his readers, and is anxious to gain and keep their sympathies, particularly those whose help was needed to free him from his current troubles. One and a half stanzas for the accusation, five for his reply, followed by a ballade double the normal length in the usual scurrilous can't-do-anything-about-it-anyway vein that he reserved for his conclusions. Here is his reply:

LX   I take it that someone says this, but it does not satisfy me at all. In effect this is how he concludes, and I think I have understood him right, that one must love respectably. The question is whether these girls, with whom I am all the time talking, were not respectable women?

LXI   Respectable they were in truth without reproach or blame. And it is true that at the beginning each one of these women took — before there was any infamy — the one a cleric, or layman, the other a monk, to extinguish the flames of love, hotter than St Anthony's fire.

LXII   Now this is the decree their lovers applied, and very obvious it is: they loved secretly, for no-one else had any share in it. Yet this love became divided, for she who had only one lover leaves him and goes her way, and prefers to love all and sundry.

LXIII   What makes them do this? I imagine, without blaming ladies' honour, that it is feminine nature that wants to love uniformly. I cannot rhyme anything else on the subject, except what is said at Rheims and Troyes, also at Lille and Saint Omer, that six workmen achieve more than three.

LXIV   Now these mad lovers are cast off and the ladies have taken wing. This is the true reward lovers get, all faith is violated in love, however sweet the kissing and hugging. With dogs, birds, weapons, love, this is a well-known truth, for one joy a hundred sorrows.

Villon's finest lyric effects have occurred in his *cris du cœur* on death and old age. In each case a feeling of revulsion leads to a lyrical climax brought to a swift end in a rumbustious, throwaway conclusion. Love cannot inspire him with such strong feelings; there is bitterness here too — his own sentimental adventures having been quite lamentable as we are soon to learn — but it is a bitterness tinged from its very beginnings with a wry humour. Love makes fools of all men, and that's that. To drive this new lesson home he has encapsulated it in another of his disrespectful, mocking pieces, where love is seen as more grotesque than tragic and the lover as a fumbling, bumble-witted clown:

And so, love as much as you please, be present at gatherings and parties, in the end you'll be no better off for it, and will only come a cropper. Foolish love makes people stupid: Solomon committed idolatry because of love, Samson lost his glasses. Very happy is he who has nothing to do with it.

Orpheus the sweet minstrel, playing flutes and bagpipes, jolly nearly killed the four-headed dog Cerberus. Narcissus, handsome and respectable, drowned in a deep well for love of his love affairs. Very happy is he who has nothing to do with it.

Sardana the noble Knight, who conquered the Kingdom of Crete, wanted, because of love, to become a woman and to spin amongst the maidens. David the King, wise prophet, forgot his fear of God, seeing well-shaped thighs being washed. Very happy is he who has nothing to do with it.

Amon, pretending to eat little tarts, wanted to dishonour and deflower his sister Thamar, that was incestuous and naughty. Herod, no trifling talk this, cut off the head of St John the Baptist for dances, jigs and little songs. Very happy is he who has nothing to do with it.

I want to talk about poor me. I was beaten like cloth in a stream, quite naked, never do I seek to hide it. Who made me chew those gooseberries were it not Katherine de Vaucelles? Noel, the third one present, got such a beating. Very happy is he who has nothing to do with it.

But will this young chap leave the girls alone? No, not even

if he were to be burned alive as a rider of broomsticks!
Sweeter are they to him than scent, and still the fool trusts
'em — be they blond, be they brunette, very happy is he
who has nothing to do with them!

Compared with the earlier developments, it is as though we have
gone straight from the first stirrings of indignation and protest
to the jesting conclusion without passing through any lyrical
climax: love's tragi-comedy does not affect Villon as much as
the tragedy of old age and death which occupies an altogether
different level in his mind. On love, too, Villon generalises, but
on this topic he sees man alone as the victim. Only once does
Villon show a woman suffering for love, and that is precisely
where he is projecting his own thoughts and feelings through the
words of his surrogate, the Belle Heaulmière, whose fidelity in
her early years was as ill-rewarded as Villon's. There is a close
parallel, and it is no coincidence. Villon usually sees love as
something of a liberation for women, a way of manipulating
men and deceiving them. He does not blame them for this: it is a
consequence of 'nature feminine'. On old age and death it was
the thought of *women's* suffering that so moved him; its
apparent absence here leaves him at the level of wry joke,
flippant expression and offhand, uproariously disrespectful
treatment of classical legend and holy scripture alike: Samson
has lost his 'glasses', Orpheus has lost his lyre and acquired in its
place flute and bagpipes, the mythical dog Cerberus has
acquired an extra head, Sardanapalus has lost half his name,
and all, including King David, his son Amnon and King Herod,
have quite lost the dignity owed to their rank (for biblical and
classical sources, see *20*B, pp.92-100). Bringing up the rearguard
of this lamentable cortège of absurd lovers is no other than
François Villon himself. These cryptic allusions to Katherine de
Vaucelles and Noel inevitably whet our appetite — who were
they and exactly what happened (see *20*B, p.98 and *6*, pp.471
and 483)? Despite much speculation and many an imaginative
novel on the subject in English or in French, no information on
this particular misadventure or on either of these characters has
survived. ('Mitaines a ces nopces telles', literally, 'such mittens

at that marriage' alludes to a quaint custom whereby guests at marriage feasts were slapped heartily on their backs to help them keep pleasant memories of the occasion in the years to come! A physical way of 'jogging' the memory!) This stanza provides a link with those following the ballade in which Villon goes on to complain of the scurvy way the woman he loved had treated him. Loyal and true, he had been tricked and deceived:

LXV   If she whom I once served with such good heart and true, from whom I had so many aches and cares and suffered so much torment, if she had told me at the beginning her intention, but not she, alas! I would have striven to escape somehow from her snares.

LXVI   Whatever I wanted to tell her she was ready to listen, neither agreeing nor disagreeing with me. Moreover, she allowed me to lie by her side and whisper in her ear, and so she kept leading me on and let me tell her everything, but it was only to deceive me.

LXVII   Deceive me she did and made me understand that one thing was another: that flour was ashes, a judge's bonnet a felt hat, that old iron dross was tin, that double aces were double threes — a deceiver always tricks others and gives chalk for cheese [lit. bladders for lanterns].

LXVIII   The sky a bronze frying pan, the clouds a calf-skin, that morning was evening, a cabbage-stump a turnip, stale beer new wine, a sow a windmill, a hangman's noose a skein of thread, a fat abbot a man-at-arms.

LXIX   So love has deceived me and driven me from pillar to post. I believe no man is so sharp, even were he as bright as the purest silver, as not to lose his linen and clothes through love, and that he would be treated as I am, who am everywhere called the man who renounces and challenges love [see *20*B, p.105].

LXX   I do renounce and challenge love and defy it through fire and blood. Because of love, death drives me to destruction and love cares not a farthing. My fiddle I've put beneath the bench, lovers I'll follow no more. If once I belonged to their ranks, I declare that I do so no longer.

LXXI For I've cast my plume to the wind. Let him follow them who expects something for it. I say nothing more about this henceforth, for I want to get on with my intention. And if someone questions me or attempts to do so, asking how I can speak ill of love, let this saying satisfy him: 'a dying man can say what he pleases.'

Although we are not to question Villon's strictures on love, we may at least point out that his attitude is poles apart from that of the courtly lover. Courtly love remains constant and unchanging however indifferent the lady, and can never be in the past, over and done with. There is nothing courtly or gallant about Villon's peeved declaration that had he really known what was on his lady-love's mind, he would have striven to escape from her clutches, and nothing romantic about his attitude towards love, although he would no doubt have agreed with Vigny's 'Et toujours, la femme est plus ou moins Dalila'. He classifies the object of his erstwhile affections amongst those who had belittled him and played him false, he who was more sinned against than sinning. Clearly his indulgent attitude towards women in general, amounting to an idealisation ('une nostalgie de pureté' in the words of one critic, see *43*, p.95) does not extend to his own personal relationships. The plaintive tones of stanzas LXV and LXVI (note the use yet again of a key word repeated several times: line 688 'abusant', lines 689 and 705 'abusé', cf. lines 313-14, 269, 273, 274, 277, 281, 287) lead to the embittered humour of the next two stanzas where the heaping-up of expressions with the same meaning underlines the strength of Villon's indignation, though all that the reader can be altogether certain about is the poet's verbal dexterity and skill in projecting an image of himself likely to evoke sympathy. The juridical and ecclesiastical authorities in Paris who had control over Villon's destiny were, of course, wholly masculine, probably with a misogynistic bias, and no doubt nodded their heads wisely over the Double Ballade's refrain and the sour reflections following that ballade. But is all this to be taken at face value? After all, it must be remembered that the unhappy, rejected lover was a fashionable figure of fifteenth-century poetry, but the conventions required him to pine sadly away because of love, not to spit defiantly in love's face, and most certainly not to refer to his lady, as Villon is soon to do (line 940), as a 'filthy bitch'! Particularly well known was Alain Chartier's *La Belle Dame sans merci*, written in 1424, to which Villon alludes later in the *Testament* (line 1805). Here is just one of Chartier's stanzas (the metrical pattern also is the one chosen by Villon):

Oh, heart harder than the blackest marble, which no mercy can enter, harder to bend than a big tree, what good do you get from being so harsh? Do you prefer to see me go to my death just to amuse you rather than, by giving a little comfort, putting off the death that threatens me?

It must also be remembered that Villon's first work, *Le Lais*, tells us in its opening lines that the cruelty and indifference of his lady threaten him with death and force him to flee (stanza V), although, as we have observed, his departure actually had altogether different, and more pressing, motives. Also, when Villon declares that, because of love, his death is near, it must be remembered that earlier in the *Testament* his real trouble is said to be one of wealth rather than health (line 74). Later, sadness and starvation are keeping him from the paths of love (line 197), although, given a chance, he would love again (line 194) and yet now (lines 713-28) he renounces love for good, whereas he declares later that he prefers to keep his love-life secret (line 1069)! Here he is the victim of the cruel Katherine de Vaucelles (assuming, and this is by no means certain, that 'celle que jadiz servoye' was indeed she, and not, already, another), and later a victim of Rose (assuming — again this is by no means certain — that this is a proper name in line 910), later still of Marthe (see acrostics to lines 950-55). Little wonder that there are as many views of Villon's love-life as there are readers of his poetry. Even the most convincingly argued interpretation is speculative. Despite the contradictions, despite the strong literary influence and hyperbolic flavour, it is impossible to assert that there was no foundation to Villon's account, even though it has been coloured by the need to contribute to the overall picture of 'le povre Villon', ill treated on all sides, deserving a better and happier fortune.

> LXXII I know the thirst of my death agonies is approaching. I spit lumps of phlegm as white as cotton and as big as tennis-balls. What's this mean? That Jeanneton no longer takes me for a young lad but for an old worn-out carthorse. I have the voice and tone of an old man yet I'm only a young simpleton.

> LXXIII Thanks be to God ... and Tacque Thibault, who made me drink so much cold water in a low place, not a high one, and suffer much ill-treatment chained up ... When I remember this, I pray for him and for all that's owed him. May God grant him, truly, truly, what I think, etc.

> LXXIV All the same, I have no evil thoughts for him in this business, or for his prosecuting counsel or presiding judge, a pleasant, kind man. I've nothing to do with the rest of them, apart from young Master Robert. I love them all together, in the same way that Lombard loves the Trinity.

The earthy unromanticism of Villon's poetry is amply revealed here: the suffering lover, fair enough, but spitting lumps of phlegm the size of tennis balls, oh dear! oh dear! The ghost of the courtly lover is laid once for all (see 6, pp.275-79) and preoccupation with the poet's physical condition, owed to quite different circumstances, takes over. How seriously his prison sentence had undermined his health is not known, but that this is all fiction seems unlikely, despite the wry, self-mocking humour revealed in the choice of words: 'valleton, cocquart, rocquart', this last one defined in Cotgrave's dictionary as 'an outworne sincaunter, one that can neither whinny, nor wag the tail' (Randle Cotgrave, *A Dictionarie of the French and English Tongues*, London, 1611). In fact Villon continues to whinny pretty effectively, even though his tail is very much between his legs. The premature ageing to which he refers brings the wheel full circle, for we are back once more with his hatred of Thibault d'Aussigny. Tacque Thibault, whose name is a transparent substitute for that of the bishop, had been a favourite of the Duke of Berry in the preceding century, hated by the people for his dissolute and cruel ways. Whatever questions are raised by the all too brief glimpses Villon gives us of his love-life, here, surely, there can be no doubt: Villon had turned his back on love and renounced it for good (or so he says: some such reaction is the invariable outcome, after all, of an unhappy affair, always meant at the time ...), but there was no renouncing this deep resentment, which lives on, as intense as ever, in the broken, uneven, clipped phraseology of these lines. The bishop's 'lieutenant' was no doubt responsible for prosecuting Villon for the (unknown) crime which led to his imprisonment, the 'official' who presided at the trial is thought to have been called Etienne Plaisance, hence the ironical choice of adjectives to describe him, and the one referred to as 'petit Robert' may have been the hangman at Orleans; more likely, however, Villon is alluding to yet another of the bishop's men at the ecclesiastical court which sentenced him to jail (see *20*B, p.112 and *6*, p.420); they constitute a trinity loved by Villon (ahem!) as though they are one and the same person, just as the twelfth-century theologian Pierre Lombard loved the Trinity (see *37*, and *20*B, pp.112-13).

LXXV   And I well remember, thanks be to God, that at the time of my departure in '56 I made out certain legacies which some people, without my consent, wanted to call 'testament'. It was their pleasure, not mine, but what can you expect? It is said commonly that no man is master of his possessions.

LXXVI   I don't say this to revoke them, even if all my

land were to be involved in it. My pity has not grown cold
for the bastard de la Barre. Along with his three bundles of
straw I give him my old matting. It will be good for him to
embrace and to keep him on his feet.

LXXVII   If it should be that somebody has not received
the legacy I made out for him, I order that after my death
he should ask my heirs for it. But who are they? Let him go
and ask Morreau, Provins and Robin Turgis. Tell them on
my behalf that I order them to see to this: they have had
even the bed on which I lie.

LXXVIII   Just one word more, for I want to begin to
make my will. In the presence of my clerk Fremin, who
hears me unless he's fallen asleep, I wish to proclaim that I
intend cursing no man in this present ordinance and I only
wish it to be published in the Kingdom of France.

LXXIX   I feel my heart growing weak and can scarcely
open my mouth any longer. Fremin, sit near my bed so
that I can't be spied on. Take ink, pen and paper at once,
write down quickly what I have to say, then have it made
known everywhere. And here's the beginning.

It is all too easy, after so much withering irony, to overlook
the importance of LXXV, a much quieter stanza. The beginning
of the *Testament* proper is announced several times (LXXVIII,
LXXIX, LXXXIV), and eventually, digressions over, it gets
under way in stanza LXXXV, but the real break occurs in stanza
LXXV. Gone now the emotion-charged verse, swept along on
the wings of massive indignation. The long train of thoughts
arising from his sufferings in prison has run its course and
petered out, diminuendo-style. His mind now reverts to his
original intention, namely, to write a literary testament for
which, he feels, a word of explanation is needed, since it is the
second one, hence the sarcastic protest at this title attached to his
first work which did not have his approval and which was clearly
going to be an embarrassment since it was needed for this fuller
work. Stanzas LXXVI and LXXVII continue the reference back

to the *Lais* and are highly topical, as are most of the legacies
soon to follow. 'Le Bastard de la Barre' was the nickname of
Perrenet Marchand, a tipstaff, that is a law enforcement officer
charged with arresting suspects. Villon had already bequeathed
to him three bundles of straw for his love-making. Now he adds
some old matting to bind round his legs in order to stand up —
too much love-making having the reputation of making men
weak at the knees! Later, stanza CVIII, he adds three loaded
dice and a pack of cards, all of which clearly suggests that
Marchand was, to say the least, no better than those he arrested.
That there are no fewer than four separate allusions to Perrenet
Marchand in Villon's work, and that he is placed here at the
head of the legatees as a sort of preliminary to the *Testament*
proper, suggests that Villon knew him all too well. Whatever the
truth of Villon's insinuations, neither the law, nor the effects of
debauchery, put an early end to the tipstaff's career since, thirty
years after Villon wrote the *Testament*, he was still in office. All
three legatees in the next stanza had apparently accepted goods
for payment until Villon had nothing left: Jean Morreau was a
meatcook, Jean de Provins a pastrycook, Robin Turgis an inn-
keeper, host of the *Pomme de Pin* in the Latin Quarter. This
second reference to his clerk Fremin (see above, p.65) keeps up
the pretence that this is a will: the ailing testator whose end is
nigh, the clerk conscientiously sitting close, noting down the
feeble and halting words — a touching picture to be taken with a
hefty grain of salt, for we are still not half-way through, and
there is much caustic, vigorous and rollicking verse to follow,
even though the lyrical heights will be scaled no more. Context
and rhyme structure have encouraged editors to take 'detester'
to mean 'to exclude from my will' (de-tester). Perhaps Villon
intended this, but nowhere else in French literature is such a
meaning found, and it is best read, therefore, as in modern
English and French, to mean 'I have no intention of hating (or
cursing) any man ...': far from being the truth, of course, but
antiphrasis is a favourite device of Villon's (compare his 'love'
for the bishop's men in stanza LXXIV). That he wanted his will
made known only in the Kingdom of France was an ironical quip
to which the passing of time has added a new and more striking

irony: Villon really intended his work for his contemporaries in Paris as the numerous topical allusions make quite clear: that it should be known only throughout the Kingdom of France was a wry joke at his own expense, something he did not really expect. The extent of the work's fame nowadays would have astonished him.

LXXX   In the name of God, Eternal Father, and of the Son whom the Virgin bore, co-eternal with God the Father and with the Holy Ghost, who saved those whom Adam condemned, and with those who had been condemned adorns the heavens ... Whoever believes this has no small merit, that dead people become little gods.

LXXXI   Dead they were, both in body and soul, in damned perdition, their bodies rotted away, their souls in flames, no matter what their status in life. However, I make an exception of the patriarchs and prophets for, as I see it, never did they feel great heat on their buttocks.

LXXXII   If someone should say to me: "What is it makes you advance this opinion so boldly, you who are not a master of theology? This is foolish presumption on your part." It is Jesus's parable concerning the rich man buried in fire, not on a soft bed, and Lazarus above him.

LXXXIII   Had he seen Lazarus's finger burning, never would he have sought coolness from it, nor would he have sought to touch the end of that finger in order to refresh his chops. Tipplers will pull wry faces in that place, who drink away their coats and shirts. Joking aside, since drink is so dear there, God save us from that place!

'In the name of God, Eternal Father' ... a conventional enough opening, parodying that of many a real will (see 6, pp.76-84), but Villon does not keep this up, breaking off in the last two lines exactly as in the opening stanza of the *Testament*, adding his own irreverent comment to the belief that after the crucifixion Christ had descended into hell in order to save those condemned by Adam's sin before His coming. Villon now embarks upon a theological disputation of a kind greatly loved by the Middle Ages, and to keep it going he soon has to resort to that favourite device of his: inventing an opponent whose objections he easily overcomes. They were all condemned except for the patriarchs and prophets. How does he know this? The parable about Lazarus (Luke, 16, 20-24) shows that Lazarus was cool and at ease while the rich man was tormented by the flames of hell. Villon carries his theological learning lightly, and, moving towards his old reputation as a *farceur* (see below, p.90), writes flippantly ('Oncques grant chault n'eurent aux fesses ...'; 'Pour raffreschir sa machouoire ...') even while showing a good knowledge of the Bible: 'reffrigere', a noun (line 818) reflects the Latin verb, 'refrigeret', of the Vulgate. The fool, rarely altogether in jest or altogether serious, such is Villon's preferred role. He is now in process of donning once more the jester's costume that he had worn for the *Lais* and, because of the circumstances described in the opening lines of the *Testament*, had neglected (to our benefit) for the first 750 lines or so of his major work.

LXXXIV   In the name of God, as I said, and of his glorious Mother, may this poem be carried without sin to its end by me, thinner than a chimera.[10] If I have not suffered from ephemeral fever, this is thanks to divine mercy. But I say nothing about other grief, and bitter loss, and thus do I begin.

LXXXV   First of all I bestow my poor soul on the glorious Trinity and commend it to Our Lady, dwelling of divinity, praying all the charity of the nine worthy orders of the heavens that by them this gift may be carried in front of the precious throne.

LXXXVI   Item, I bequeath and leave my body to our great mother, the earth. The worms won't find much fat

[10] The mythical monster known as a chimera was not thin, but may have been so represented, with protruding ribs, in carvings on Notre Dame de Paris, and the Sainte-Chapelle, so Villon's reference here is to something seen, not read. See *20*B, pp.123-24.

on it, hunger has waged too harsh a war on it. Now may it
be given up rapidly. From the earth it came, to the earth it
returns. All things, unless I'm much mistaken, willingly
return to their source.

LXXXVII   Item, and to my more than father, Master
Guillaume de Villon, who has been sweeter to me than a
mother to a child out of swaddling clothes. He has got me
out of many a scrape, and does not rejoice over this one. I
beg him on my knees to leave all the rejoicing to me.

LXXXVIII   I give him my library and the Tale of the
Devil's Fart which Master Guy Tabarye copied out, he
who is a truthful man. It's in loose covers under a table.
Although it's a crude piece of work the subject matter is so
noteworthy that it makes up for all its shortcomings.

At last, stanza LXXXIV announces the beginning, fights off an
embryonic digression on his thin and feverish plight — as
though he has thought to himself: 'enough of that' — and we are
under way: his soul, as in a conventional will, to the Trinity,
though the invocation of the nine worthy orders of the heavens
is carrying things rather far, his body to the earth, with yet
another reminder of his deprivations, then the first legacy of this
main series for those he is leaving behind, reserved for
Guillaume de Villon. The gratitude expressed in stanza
LXXXVII rings true, but the legacy sounds to be a joke. What
library is François likely to have possessed (see 6, pp.237-38)? As
for the Tale of the Devil's Fart, the title is sufficiently revealing
in itself. In fact the Devil's Fart, well known to Parisians in
Villon's day, was a large stone which had stood in front of the
house of Mademoiselle de Bruyères in the Ile de la Cité. In the
early '50s, during Villon's days at University, the students
'captured' it and it became a bone of contention between the
students and the authorities, held first by one side, then the
other (see 6, pp.145-51). Villon may well have written a farcical
account of these goings-on, and — who knows? — if Guillaume
de Villon had a sense of humour, maybe he would have enjoyed
reading it. Whether or not he read it, if so with what feelings, we

shall never know. Even if Guy Tabarye — Villon's all too 'truthful' accomplice (see above p.27) — did copy it out, it has unfortunately not survived. Some commentators suppose that it never actually existed. The resemblance of the dialectal 'cayeulx' (here substituted for 'cahiers') to the name Colin de Cayeux, who, like Tabarye, was one of Villon's accomplices in the robbery of the Collège de Navarre, suggests that the stanza is a veiled allusion to the robbery (see *20*B, p.129). If so, one looks in vain for a note of regret at something that can only have added to Guillaume's woes. Five years earlier, in the *Lais*, Guillaume had already headed the list of François's legatees, and on that occasion had received his reputation — not likely to have been of great worth! — his tents and pavilion, i.e. goods and chattels, also, surely of little worth. The flippancy of Villon's legacies to Guillaume is puzzling (see *16*, I, p.14, note 3) and cannot be explained by the very theme of a mock will since the legacy that follows, to his mother, is entirely serious. A likely explanation must lie with the relationship between the two, even though we can only surmise: an easy, close familiarity, exonerating Villon from any need to show respect, even allowing him a quip or two at the chaplain's expense: no need of reassurances, each was sure of the other. Despite his regrets and disappointment, Guillaume knew, and accepted, François for what he was.

LXXXIX   Item, I give to my poor mother, to greet Our Lady (my mother has suffered bitter grief, God knows, and many a sadness on my account) — I have no other castle or fortress to which I can retire in body and soul, when evil distress assails me, neither has my mother, the poor woman —

Ballade to be used as a Prayer to Our Lady

Lady of Heaven, ruler of earth, Empress of the marshes of Hell, receive me, your humble Christian, that I may be included amongst your elect, although I was never of any worth. Your virtues, my lady, my mistress, far outweigh my sins, and without those virtues no soul can deserve or receive the heavens: I am no liar in this: in this faith I want to live and die.

Tell your Son that I am his. By him may my sins be absolved. May he pardon me as he did St Mary of Egypt or the clerk Théophile who was freed and absolved by you even though he had made a pact with the devil.[11] Preserve me from ever doing that, Virgin who, while remaining intact, bore the sacrament that we celebrate at mass. In this faith I want to live and die.

I am a poor, ancient old woman who knows nothing and could never read. At the church, of which I am a parishioner, I see painted paradise where there are harps and lutes and a hell where the damned are boiled. One gives me fear, the other joy and happiness. Give me the joy, noble goddess, to whom all sinners must have recourse, overwhelmed with faith, without pretence or sloth. In this faith I want to live and die.

You bore, worthy Virgin, princess, Jesus reigning for all eternity. The Omnipotent, taking on our feeble form, left the heavens and came to our help, offered to death his very dear youth. Such is Our Lord, such do I confess him to be. In this faith I want to live and die.

This poem to be recited by his mother is one of Villon's rare serious personal notes on behalf of an individual other than himself, token no doubt of the depth and truth of his feelings towards his mother. It is a splendid and devout prayer built around its refrain, whose unchanging yet ever more insistent recurrences skilfully underline the steadfastness of his mother's faith. The third stanza, one of Villon's vivid thumbnail sketches, portrays his mother as she gazes in awe at the paintings in church of heaven and hell, hoping for the former, in dread of the latter. Clearly, there is not the slightest trace of banter here. The

[11] Both St Mary and Théophile were the subjects of works by the thirteenth-century Parisian poet Rutebeuf, which Villon may have read. The Théophile legend, resembling that of Faust, figures in carvings on the Northern porch of Notre Dame, which Villon had no doubt seen.

intention to honour and please his mother and to make amends for his many misdemeanours, is obvious enough, and his pride in the poem is shown by the 'signature', that is, the acrostics spelling out his name in the envoi. This ballade also represents the first use by Villon in the *Testament* of decasyllabic verse compared with his more usual octosyllables. The *Testament* contains a further six ballades using the decasyllabic line (against a total of eight in octosyllabics, most of which appear to have been written expressly for the *Testament*, whereas the decasyllabic ballades may well have been earlier compositions), a further eight occur in the small collection usually referred to as *Les Poésies diverses* or *Les Poèmes variés* (against six in octosyllabic verse in that same set), and five in the series of *Ballades en jargon* (as against four in octosyllabic verse, two in heterometric verse) as published by A. Lanly (*18*). The decasyllabic had been the preferred measure of the medieval French epic, the octosyllabic that of courtly romance. There is no clear line of demarcation between the two for Villon: some of his most light-hearted verse is in the longer measure as well as some of his most solemn verse, as in this ballade for his mother. Apart from length, the two differed in that the decasyllabic had a caesura, that is, an accent falling on the fourth syllable with an optional sense pause after it (the fourth syllable, in consequence, had to carry a natural stress: for example, it could never be a preposition such as *de*, or the first syllable of a word such as *devoir*, *heureux*; exceptionally, in lyric verse, the caesura accent could fall on a final weak 'e' — the so-called 'lyric caesura' — as in line 12 of this ballade). The poet could write:

En ceste *foy* je vueil vivre et mourir

but not

En ceste creance je vueil mourir

Similarly

Dame du ciel, regente terrienne

could not be recast as

Regente du ciel, reine terrienne

Acceptable, on the other hand, despite the absence of sense pause, is

De luy soient mes pechiez aboluz

A good line brings together caesura and sense pause, thereby causing the fourth syllable to stand out, particularly striking when it is a monosyllable, as happens in no fewer than two-thirds of the lines in this poem: Dame du *ciel* ... Recevez *moy* ... Les biens de *vous* ... Sont trop plus *grans* ... Sans lesquelz *biens* ... N'avoir les *cieulx* ... En ceste *foy* ... A vostre *Filz* ... Pardonne *moy* ... etc.

XC   Item, to my love, my darling rose, I leave neither my heart, nor my liver. She'd prefer something else, although she has plenty of money. A large silken purse, full of crowns, deep and wide. But may he be hanged, myself included, who will leave her a crown or a farthing.

XCI   For she has plenty enough without me. But I don't care about it, my greatest cares in the matter are over and done with, it doesn't give me a hot backside any longer. I leave it to the heirs of Michault who was called the Good Lover. Pray for him, go on a quick visit: he lies at Saint Satur near Sancerre.

XCII   All the same, to pay my debt to Love more than to her — for never could I get a single spark of encouragement from her. I don't know if she's treated all men as scurvily, I don't greatly care, but, by the lovely St Mary, it's no laughing matter, as far as I'm concerned. [See *20*B, p.138]

XCIII   I send her this ballade, ending throughout in the letter R. Who shall take it to her? Let me see now ... It shall be Pernet de la Barre, provided that if on the way he encounters the damsel with the twisted nose, he shall say to her without further ado: You filthy bitch, where have you been?

Ballade to his lady-love

False beauty which cost me so dear, harsh in reality, hypocritical sweetness, love harder in the mouth than iron, which, being certain of my undoing, I can call deceitful charm, the death of a poor heart, hidden pride which puts people to death, pitiless eyes, does not strict justice demand that a poor man be helped, not crushed?

It would have been better for me to look elsewhere for help, that would have been an honourable course for me. Nothing could have got me out of this mess, now I've got to run away in disgrace. Help, help, one and all![12] What's it all mean? Shall I die without striking a blow, or does pity not want, according to this text of mine, that a poor man be helped, not crushed?

A time will come which will make your bloom dry up, go yellow and wither away. I would have a good laugh then, if I was capable of it. But no, it would be madness. I shall be old, you ugly and with no complexion. Now drink up while the stream still flows. Don't give this grief to all men: a poor man must be helped and not crushed.

Loving prince, of lovers the greatest, I would not wish to incur your ill-favour, but every noble heart must, for Our Lord's sake, help a poor man, not crush him.

What a violent contrast, the moment Villon turns from his mother to the one who was presumably, after her, the second most important woman in his life: the dignity and steadfastness of the one condemn the dissoluteness and disloyalty of the other. Villon's verse at this juncture is filled with erotic allusions, transparent enough (remember what Villon has said about Perrenet Marchand's reputation (see above p.75), hence the choice of him as messenger!) apart from 'escu ne targe' in line

---

[12] A literal translation is very difficult here. 'Le grant haro' was a Norman cry of alarm in times of danger, e.g. on being attacked by the English. 'Le petit haro' appears to be a Villon invention.

916: both meaning 'shields', also 'coins', also 'phallus'. In line 925 Saint Satur may simply be chosen for its resemblance to 'satyr', also for the hissing effect of the line which conveys something of Villon's hatred and derision. As for his ending every line of the ballade with the letter 'r' (still a rolled 'r' in Villon's day, with a more vigorous sound to it than the so-called Parisian 'r' of present-day French), it was traditionally associated in medieval times with resentment and anger, so representing here Villon's feelings rather than his love's faithlessness. The ballade may well have been composed before the stanzas introducing it since they put the affair in the past whereas the ballade puts it in the present or the immediate past. The tone of the ballade is less harsh, with nothing as unpleasant as 'orde paillarde', even though expressions such as 'faulse beauté', 'amour dure', 'charme felon', 'orgueil mussé', 'yeulx sans pitié' are caustic enough, more so in their cumulative effect. The third stanza's appeal to his lady-love to think again, is clearly more a matter of the old 'carpe diem' convention than of conviction: if 'de ma deffaçon seur' is true, then the affair, at the time of writing, is as good as over. The poem makes use of acrostics, the initial letters of the first stanza spelling out François, the second Marthe, the third looks like a half-hearted attempt to spell his own name (Viilvon), as though he set out with this intention, but lost interest. Biographical details aside, what are we to make of this poem? To judge Villon's poetry objectively, without constant reference to his life and feelings, is notoriously difficult because of its very nature. It is a jaded, end-of-affair poem for a jaded, end-of-era century when the old courtly conceptions had worn threadbare and no new life had as yet been breathed into French poetry, which clung on to fading memories and ideals in which it no longer believed. Inasmuch as he is a poet of love at all, Villon is a poet of love's ending, never beginning. That a platonic affair can offer much happiness is an idea utterly foreign to him and his whole post-war era, intent — as are all such eras — on getting all it can from whatever physical pleasures life has to offer. Keen awareness of life's brevity and fickleness — has Villon ever been surpassed in this respect? — sharpens the interest in all things sensual.

XCIV Item, to Master Ythier Marchant, to whom I formerly bequeathed my sword, I give, provided he sets it to music, this lay containing ten lines, a *De Profundis* to be set to the lute, for his former love whose name I do not tell, for he would hate me for evermore.

Lay

Death, I cry out against your harshness, for you have snatched from me my mistress, and are still not assuaged, unless you keep me languishing. Never since have I had strength or vigour. But what harm did she do you in life, Death?

We two had but one heart. If it is dead, then I too must be without life, or live on lifeless, like pictures, in the mind only, Death.

Ythier Marchant is known to have been the same age as Villon, very likely a fellow-student. He found employment with the King's brother but was later arrested and put to death for conspiracy. This 'lay', or rondeau, is reproduced here as it appears in the manuscripts. (The full, musical version of the rondeau, which is what Villon requests, called for the repetition of the first two lines *in their entirety* instead of the single word 'Mort' in the middle of the poem, and of the first four lines at the end. Whether the *read* version was necessarily treated in this way is quite another question. The fact that some contemporary rondeaux do not make sense with the full repetition suggests that the style was evolving at this period in which lyric poetry was being weaned from music, with which it had for long been associated.) It is the only poem in which Villon speaks of love effectively — 'Deux estions et n'avions qu'un cœur' is a memorable and beautiful line — and without spite or sourness, but it is on the death of a mistress, and, as stanza XCIV reveals, another man's mistress.

*   *   *   *

The next thirty-one stanzas distribute satirical legacies to various of Villon's contemporaries in Paris, some of them prominent figures, many of them minor officials concerned with the law, finance or administration. References often remain obscure because they assume a knowledge of the person and the circumstances alluded to, proof that Villon was writing for a very restricted circle indeed. On the first such legatee, Jean Cornu (stanza XCV) Villon's most recent editors comment: 'Comme les données extra-textuelles (circonstances, personnages, etc.) nous échappent, nous avons de la peine à comprendre pleinement le texte lui-même' (see *20*B, p.147), thereby echoing Marot's comment on the *Testament* as a whole, made three hundred years earlier and less than a hundred years after Villon was writing: 'Quant à l'industrie de ses lays qu'il feit en ses testaments, pour suffisamment la congnoistre et entendre, il faudroit avoir esté de son temps à Paris, et avoir congneu les lieux, les choses et les hommes dont il parle: la memmoire desquelz tant plus se passera, tant moins se congnoistra icelle industrie de ses lays dictz'. Research in the Paris archives by Pierre Champion and others (see *5*, *6* and *7*) has prevented this prediction from coming true. In fact we know more about Villon's legatees than did Clément Marot, but even so, his comments remain valid.

As examples of the text's obscurity owed to this extreme topicality: Master Jean Cornu, whom the archives show to have been variously a tax-collector, secretary to the King, and, at the time Villon was writing, an administrator in the provost's office, 'since he has always helped me in my hour of need' (lines 993-94, meaning very likely the opposite!) receives the garden which Villon rented from Master Pierre Bobignon (public prosecutor at the Châtelet) provided he repairs the door and straightens up the gable (lines 994-98). The lack of a door accounted for Villon's loss there of a paving-stone and a hoe handle: Cornu is sure to spend a bloody awful night there ('sanglante nuyt') and sleep on the ground (lines 998-1005). Maître Pierre de Saint-Amand (another of the King's secretaries and clerk in the Treasury), whose wife had called Villon a beggar, receives, in place of the White Horse Inn and the Mule, bequeathed to him in the *Lais* (stanza XII; possibly only the tavern signs — often stolen by students in Villon's day, or rearranged — were involved), a mare and a red donkey (stanza XCVII), a reflection, possibly, on the worthy couple's infertility. Denis Hesselin (tax inspector) receives fourteen barrels of wine from Robin Turgis: he is to water it down if there is any risk of his getting drunk (stanza XCVIII). Was he in fact a teetotaller? Or fond of the bottle, on the contrary? Or, since he was responsible for taxes on wine, would his receiving such a large quantity (3780 litres, to be precise!) have been an embarrassment to him? Whatever the truth, like Perrenet Marchand and numbers of Villon's legatees, he was still in office years after Villon had disappeared from the scene for good. Guillaume Charruau, a fellow-student of Villon's in years gone by, receives Villon's sword formerly bequeathed to Ythier Marchand: I'll say nothing, adds Villon, about the scabbard (stanza XCIX); commentators have no difficulty in seeing erotic undertones therein. Villon's solicitor Fournier receives four handfuls ('havees') from his purse, of what is not specified (stanza C). Loose change? Meagre harvest if so! Air? Or does 'havees' suggest Latin 'ave', greetings, and nothing else? Altogether Villon names over fifty beneficiaries in addition to several groups such as the mendicant friars. The tone is generally one of banter, the bequest more likely to contribute to its receiver's discomfiture than anything else.

A change occurs after some thirty stanzas, when Jean Cotart, mentioned already in stanza V (see above, p.19), who had died shortly before Villon was released from prison and who had defended him against a charge of slandering Denise (who was she? No information is available), receives, or rather is commemorated by, a ballade celebrating his prowess as a carouser, so thirsty that he could not even spit as far as the ground, each stanza working up to the refrain 'L'ame du bon feu maistre Jean Cotart', 'the soul of the good, late, Master Jean Cotart'. Occasionally serious, more often satirical, Villon often keeps us guessing. His habit of saying one thing and meaning the opposite does not clarify matters: readers were at one time moved by his seemingly kind references to three poor orphans (stanza CXXVII) now known to have been three rich old moneylenders! The next ballade after the Jean Cotart one was to be recited by Robert d'Estouteville, provost of Paris, to his wife Ambroise de Loré (in fact the provost was dismissed from office in 1460, the year before the *Testament* was written. Was the ballade written before or after his demise? Latest research puts it after, see *20*B, p.200). It is universally regarded nowadays as a panegyric, albeit somewhat heavy-handed, of conjugal love (see *20*B, p.200, *16*, I, p.217, *6*, pp.297-300) though the possibility of a mocking intention has not been overlooked (see *43*, p.96). In favour of such an interpretation are the following features:

1. Villon reports that the provost won his wife at a tournament (we have only his word for this; see *20*B, p.198), the sort of incongruous detail he delights in (like the monarch whose claim to glory, in Villon's eyes, is that he had a purple face, *Testament*, lines 365-68) and a wry comment, to say the least, on the contingencies of love.

2. Having won his wife in the field, the provost treats her like one: I don't waste the seed I sow in your field, he is made to say, since the fruit resembles me (lines 1398-1401).

3. Each stanza has an agrarian flavour: birds sing and mate in the first, laurel and olive provide the symbolism of the second (see *32*, pp.85-93), seed is sown, the land dug and tilled (a common erotic metaphor), in the third.

Villon is very soon to reveal his true attitude towards the supposed joys of country life, as we shall see. Moreover, those who believe that the biblical basis of this farming imagery (the sower of the seed etc.) guarantees the seriousness of the poem are overlooking the *Double Ballade* and other passages (e.g. stanza LXXXI). Less than a hundred lines later, in another ballade, bequeathed to Master Andry Courault, King's counsellor in the Treasury, Villon slams the fashionable idea that the ideal life is a rustic one: a well-carpeted room, with a roaring fire, an endless supply of spiced wine, a naked, white and smooth-skinned woman at your side, that is Villon's ideal, far better, he feels, than any outdoor life ... Ideal life, also, and of a not too different kind, in the famous *Ballade de la Grosse Margot*, where Villon is a pimp living on Margot's earnings. (Some commentators think that this is pure fiction, inspired by the brothel of that name in the Paris of Villon's day. The latest editors, however, believe that Margot was a real person, *20*B, p.221, while Favier believes that the episode is real enough whatever the prostitute's name, *6*, p.314.) The verse captures the noisy and smelly atmosphere of the bordel:

> Then peace descends, and she blows me a mighty fart, more bloated than a poisonous dungbeetle. Laughing, she slaps her fist on the top of my head: 'Get on with it' she says, and whacks my thigh. Both drunk, wc sleep like logs. Waking up with a rumbling belly, she climbs on me so I don't spoil her fruit. I groan beneath her weight, she squashes me flatter than a plank. Her obscene ways kill my desire, in this brothel where we hold our court.

The concluding lines of this ballade, which carry Villon's name in acrostics, give a very clear-sighted condemnation of the pair of them. The voice of Villon's conscience? Or a make-of-it-what-you-please defiance to the very end? The reader must decide:

> Whether it blows, hails or freezes, my living's assured. I'm debauched, the debauched woman follows mc. Which is better? We're two of a kind, the one is worth the other, a bad rat for a bad cat. We love filth, filth pursues us. We flee from honour, it flees from us, in this brothel where we hold our court.

In one short, characteristically vivid and intense passage, the coarseness and laughter are halted. Having mentioned the Cimetière aux Innocents in Paris, Villon breaks off and reflects once more, faint echo of the *Testament*'s early stanzas, on the brevity and futility of life:

> CLXI   This is no laughing matter, no game. What good did it do them to be wealthy and sleep in ornate beds, to gulp wine down and fatten up their paunches, to make merry at dances and parties and to be ready for such things

at all times? All such pleasures come to an end, only the sin remains.

CLXII   When I consider the skulls piled up in the charnel houses, they were all King's counsellors or members of the royal household, or else they were all streetporters. I might as well say the one as the other, for whether they were bishops or lamp-lighters, I can't see any difference now.

CLXIII   And those who bowed to each other in their lives, some of them reigning, feared and served by the others, I see them all there brought to nothing, all together in an untidy heap. Gone now their influence and titles: none is called clerk or master now.

CLXIV   Now they are dead, may God have their souls! As for the bodies, they have rotted away. Even if they were lords and ladies, fed tenderly, gently, on cream, frumenty and rice, their bones too turn to dust, merriment and laughter mean nothing to them now. May the sweet Jesus absolve them!

Serious in tone, too, the rondeau for his friend Jacquet Cardon, celebrating Villon's release from prison: 'Ou j'ay laissié presque la vie', serious, too, his explanation as to why this 'povre petit escollier / Qui fut nommé Françoys Villon' should choose to end his major work in banter and mockery:

At least the memory of me shall remain, as it now is, of a good clown.

Hoist with his own petard, the author of the *Lais* cannot have been known as a serious lyric poet. 'Might as well end as I've begun', is his fatalistic conclusion. But for him there is no clear dichotomy. When serious he has many a joking aside, and in the midst of coarse laughter a sober thought can intrude. Nobody has provided a better summing up than Villon himself: 'Je ris en pleurs'. (True of many a poet, says Siciliano, see *9*, p.106, note 3, also *35*, pp.115-16.) And is it not extraordinary, at the same time magnificent, that the author of some of the finest lyric poetry ever composed in the French language should take his leave of us, and of life, with his glass raised to his lips, quaffing a draught of the best red wine:

> Here's what he did at his departure: he drank a draught of best red wine, when he was about to leave this world.

Defiant, unrepentant, incorrigible to the last.

2. Miscellaneous Poems: 'Le Débat de Villon et de son cœur' and 'La Ballade des pendus'

Apart from the *Lais* and the *Testament*, sixteen miscellaneous poems by Villon have survived, mostly ballades (see Introduction). Their most recent editors divide them into three groups: *Les Poèmes de Blois-Orléans, Les Ballades de morale versifiée, Prison et potence* (see *20*D, pp.51-52). The first were written at Charles d'Orléans's court in Blois some time between Villon's departure from Paris in 1456 and his imprisonment at Meung-sur-Loire in 1461, probably in December 1457 and January 1458 (see *20*D, p.51). Longest of this series of seven poems is a laboured piece of flattery in celebration of the birth of the duke's daughter, Marie, on 19 December 1457: *Louange à Marie d'Orléans*. Also in this group are the *Ballade des contradictions* on a theme supplied by the Duke of Orleans and expressed in the first line: 'Je meurs de soif auprès de la fontaine' (see *20*D, pp.68-69) and a 'macaronic' ballade in a mixture of Latin and French. Of particular interest is the fact that in the principal Orleans manuscript (see *20*C, p.35) these three poems are copied out in a hand found nowhere else, believed to be that of Villon himself. Turning over the pages, he could have set eyes on a macaronic ballade by the duke, hence the idea for his own poem. However, he was clearly in a hurry: the ink is pale, suggesting that the pen was not being dipped fully into the inkwell, a line has been missed out and added in the margin, there are repetitions and careless use of language (see *20*D, pp.53-57). The second group, from the same period between the *Lais* and the *Testament*, comprises three moralising poems, the *Ballade de bon conseil*, the *Ballade contre les ennemis de France* (of uncertain attribution), and the *Ballade de fortune*. The final group, six poems in all, was written about the same time as the *Testament*, shortly after his release from prison, including the *Débat de Villon et de son cœur*, while some, the last poems we have from him, were a little later, belonging to the period December 1462-January 1463, the *Quatrain*, the *Louange et requête à la cour*, and the *Question au clerc du guichet*, all three relating to the death sentence passed on him and its remission, on 5 January 1463 (n.s.) to one of a ten-year banishment from Paris. That the famous *Ballade des pendus* belongs to this last group is often assumed, and seems likely, but remains uncertain (see *20*D, p.110).

All these poems have their merit, but only two can rank with the first thousand lines of the *Testament*, contributing to Villon's reputation as France's greatest lyric poet. They also add to our understanding of Villon's particular genius, and his gifts as a poet. They are the *Débat de Villon et de son cœur*, and the *Ballade des pendus*.

Villon's Debate with his Heart

What's that I hear? — *It is I* — Who? — *Your heart, which is only holding on by a tiny thread. I have no strength left, no substance, no blood, when I see you squatting alone like this, like a wretched dog crouched in a corner.* — Why is it so? — *Because of your foolish love of pleasure.* — What does it matter to you? — *I get the displeasure of it.* — Leave me in peace. — *Why?* — I'll think about it. — *When will that be?* — When I'm out of childhood. — *I tell you no more.* — And I'll do without it.

What do you think you are? — A man of worth. — *You're 30 years old.* — That's a good age for a mule. — *Is it childhood?* — Nay. — *So it's madness that has seized hold of you?* — Where's it seized me by? The collar? — *You know nothing.* — Oh yes I do. — *What?* — Fly in milk. One's white, the other black, that's distance. — *Is that all?* — What do you want me to argue about? If it's not enough, I'll begin again. — *You're ruined.* — I'll resist that. — *I tell you no more.* — And I'll do without it.

I get the sorrow, you the ache and pain. If you were a poor, stupid idiot, you would have some excuse. But you don't care, it's all the same to you, good or bad. Either

*your head's harder than a stone, or this misfortune pleases
you more than honour. What will you reply to this
argument?* — I'll be free of it when I die. — *God, what
comfort!* — What wise eloquence! — *I tell you no more.*
— And I'll do without it.

Where does this trouble come from? — It comes from my
misfortune: when Saturn prepared my burden for me, he
imposed these terms, I believe. — *That's madness: you're
his master and you act as his servant! See what Solomon
wrote in his book: a wise man, he said, has power over the
planets and their influence.* — I don't believe a word of
that. What they have made of me, I shall remain. —
Whatever's that you say? — In truth, it's my belief. — *I
tell you no more.* — And I'll do without it.

Do you want to live? — God grant me the power to do so!
— *You need ...* — What? — *Remorse, read without end.*
— What should I read? — *Read for wisdom, leave fools
alone.* — I'll take good heed. — *Now remember it!* — I've
got it well in mind. — *Don't wait until it becomes a
torture. I tell you no more.* — And I'll do without it.

In this ballade as elsewhere in his work, Villon's claim to
originality lies not in the form but in the contents. Ballades in
the form of a dialogue go back at least to the time of Eustache
Deschamps in the late fourteenth century, earlier if we include
the *jeux-partis*, of Provençal origin, in which two poets debate
together. The earliest printed edition (1489) gives, as title, *Le
Debat du cueur et du corps dudit Villon*. In modern parlance it is
a debate between the poet and his conscience ('cueur' of line 1).
The promptings of his inner voice have already made themselves
heard in the *Testament* (stanza XXXVI) but there they were
comforting rather than chiding. This tense and closely argued
poem gives the lie to the claim that no individual could be both
serious and jesting within the confines of one work as Villon is in
the *Testament*, and that, consequently, the *Testament* must
consist of two works, the first part, now dubbed the *Regrets*
(specifically, lines 89-328) having been composed many years

after the rest (see *46, 47, 33, 36*). This *Débat* shows that Villon is conscious of his own duality as sober thoughts on how life should be spent alternate with light-hearted, why-bother jestings. The conscience opens with bitter remonstrances which allude either to Villon's being in prison (lines 4-5), or to his being in hiding shortly after release from prison. These reproaches are first of all rejected outright, then countered with an offhand promise to give some thought to the matter when he's out of childhood. The flippancy of this rejoinder emerges more clearly in the second stanza when we learn that he is thirty years old (cf. *Testament*, line 1), and carries on in three further dismissals of the prickings of conscience. In the third stanza the conscience's onslaught gathers force, occupying eight of the ten lines, at last provoking an attempt at a serious reply: 'it's all a matter of fate, nothing I can do will change things'; the same argument as in the *Testament* (lines 145-48). In the envoi, while the name Villon is being spelled out in acrostics, a dramatic change takes place, and the conscience appears to triumph. 'Do you want to live?' (an echo, perhaps, of 'vive en bien', *Testament*, line 107). So eager is the reaction to this question that the conscience is interrupted before it can spell out the remedy, and is interrupted again while giving it: have remorse, read books of wisdom, abandon foolish company. The tenor of these last lines changes the meaning of the rejoinder in the final refrain. Following on from 'Bien j'y adviseray' and 'J'en ay bien souvenance', the last 'Et je m'en passeray' implies that enough has been said and that further advice is superfluous. To read it otherwise at this juncture would be to make of it a *non-sequitur* (see *6*, p.437 and *20*D, p.123). We have moved from sullen rejection, through flippancy and fatalism to a promise to heed the advice given and to strive for a better future. As with the beginning of the *Testament*, one may suspect Villon (given his circumstances at the time of his imprisonment and soon after) to be writing with an eye on the likely effect of his poem on those reading it ('not such a bad fellow after all ...') and, to be sure, nothing entitles us to say that he is 'sincere'; but the artistry of the poem is very great, as is its authenticity, the conflict of feelings reflecting a common enough human predicament, the regret owed to the difference between what we are, and what, with greater effort, we could have been.

* * * *

Ballade of the Hanged Men

Brother men who live after us, do not have your hearts hardened against us, for if you have pity on us, God will the sooner have mercy on you. You can see us strung up here, five or six of us. As for the flesh which we fed only too well, for a long time now it has been eaten up and rotten, and we, the bones, are turning to ashes and dust. Let no-one mock at our plight, but pray to God that he will absolve us all.

If we call you brothers, you must not feel disdain, although we were killed by justice. You know all the same that not all men are of good sense. Ask forgiveness for us, since we are no more, from the Son of the Virgin Mary, so that his grace is not dried up for us, preserving us from the thunderbolt of hell. We are dead, let no-one harry us, but pray to God that he will absolve us all.

The rain has soaked and washed us and the sun dried and blackened us. Magpies and crows have hollowed out our eyes, torn away our beard and eyebrows. Never at any time are we still. This way and that, as the wind turns, it shifts us around as it pleases, never stopping, pecked by birds until we are more pitted than thimbles. Do not join our brotherhood, then, but pray to God that he will absolve us all.

Prince Jesus who is Lord of all, take care lest Hell have dominion over us. Let us have nothing to do with that place, nothing to owe it. Men, here there is no mockery, but pray to God that he will absolve us all.

The *Testament*'s reminder that, however different our lives, death awaits us all (stanzas XXXIX-XLI) is carried further in this direct appeal. The bonds of humanity reach even beyond the barrier of death — 'Brother men who live after us ...' In this grim flight of fancy not far removed from the realities of his existence (even if not composed, as it may have been, under actual sentence of death), Villon sees himself as a skeleton on the gallows amongst others. The first person plural, rather than singular, is significant: not simply a personal supplication by 'le povre Villon', but a prayer from the dead to the living, a last desperate appeal for mercy, tolerance and understanding even for the most wicked of men, and a pathetic plea not to laugh at the blackened remains, swinging in the wind. It is a humanitarian poem, also a very Christian one.

In the *Ballade des pendus*, one of Villon's outstanding qualities is revealed: the *visual* effect, the ability to conjure up a whole scene in a few lines, sometimes in a few words. It is Villon's seeing eye that accounts for his pre-eminence, not his reading, not the depth of his feeling, whatever that might mean; many a lesser poet no doubt had feelings every bit as acute. Villon has observed and captured in his verse what was reflected in his retina: here the rotting corpses on the public gallows, gruesome enough, less so than the sweating contorsions of the dying man depicted in the *Testament* (stanzas XL and XLI). No reference there or here to sounds, but only to what the eye sees. More often it is observation of the living, caught in one or two lines: the bishop making the sign of the cross as he walks through the streets, the beggars eying the bread in the shopwindows, the friars at their tables laden with good food, reaching out to pour their own drinks, the weaver running a handful of burning straw across his cloth to remove loose ends, the labourers carrying blocks of stone up to the masons, the old women squatting around a tiny fire, reminiscing about the good old days, younger women 'assises / Sur le bas du ply de leurs robes' (*Testament*, lines 1543-44: this singling out of one picturesque detail is part of the technique), gossiping together in groups of two or three, Villon's mother as she stands in church, gazing in awe at the paintings of heaven and hell, while the reader can picture Villon himself meditating over the skulls piled

high in the charnel-houses. Two recent discoveries are
significant: his reference to himself as 'thinner than a chimera'
(*Testament*, line 828) is not a literary reminiscence, but a visual
one inspired by carvings on Notre-Dame de Paris, and the
heroines Bietrix and Aliz, named in the *Ballade des dames* are
depicted in manuscripts of the text concerned, *Hervis de Metz*
(see below, p.99), in illuminations with their names underneath,
in rubrics.[13] This capacity for depicting what he has seen —
nowhere more effectively than in the *Ballade des pendus* —
contributes much to the feeling that this is not a bookish,
literature-type of poetry, belonging, as does so much French
poetry from the twelfth to the twentieth century, to a literary
school of some sort, but a poetry that is still living and lived, a
poetry that can still make great impact on its readers, hence the
frequent references to Villon as 'first of us all'.

[13] Not to imply that Villon had not read the text, but the illuminations pick out
these two characters, as does Villon in his poem.

Conclusion

Modern Interpretations

Every century since the sixteenth has had its own ideas on François Villon and his poetry. In the history of French literary criticism, Villon's is the longest unbroken record, his predecessors having been largely forgotten until the revival of interest in the medieval period owed to the Romantic movement. Only the seventeenth century saw no new edition of Villon's poetry (see *10*). He remained, however, a shadowy, enigmatic figure until the biographical details that had long remained buried in the archives of Paris were brought to light in 1877 in Auguste Longnon's *Etude biographique sur François Villon, d'après les documents inédits conservés aux Archives Nationales*. A veritable explosion of interest followed. In the first half of the twentieth century over fifty editions of Villon's works appeared (see *2*). Research continued to be focussed on Villon's life and on his legatees. Despite the industry and diligence of so many distinguished scholars, (apart from Longnon and Foulet, those deserving special mention, and whose works are listed in *2*, include August Vitu, Marcel Schwob, Louis Thuasne, Pierre Champion), many an enigma remains. During this same period numerous details of this text so tightly packed with allusions were explained (*Villoniana* became a standard title for such articles), or hypotheses put forward which contribute to our understanding of the text.

In the second half of the twentieth century, the desire to find something new to say when the archives have been squeezed dry, and the conviction (mistaken) that the text itself has nothing more to yield[14] have led to investigation of what is sometimes

---

[14] Some scholars are still active in this sphere which is by no means exhausted, notably J. Dufournet, see *29* and *31*. Even now some long-standing mysteries are being cleared up. Only in 1981 were Bietris and Alis, referred to in the *Ballade des dames*, identified, see *44*.

called the infratext. That the text sometimes has a hidden meaning, the opposite of what it appears to say, is well established,[15] that Villon sometimes uses the initial letters of the lines of his ballades to spell out his name as a kind of indelible signature is also well known. Such features, along with Lucien Foulet's suggestion that the expression 'remply sur les chantiers' (*Testament*, line 199) is a reference to Villon's friend Ythiers Marchand (see *11*, p.155), have encouraged scholars to delve deeply in order to find hitherto unsuspected anagrams and meanings. Such delvings testify to the individual scholar's ingenuity more than to anything else, but some substantial works have appeared recently, damaging and mischievous because they present as fact what is no more than surmise, or fantasy. Dr Ethel Seaton's *Studies in Villon, Vaillant and Charles d'Orléans* (Oxford, 1957) takes the initial and post-caesural letters of Villon's ballades, and proceeds, Scrabble-like, to build from them various names, either taken from elsewhere in Villon's poetry (there is a wide choice, after all!) or names of contemporaries certainly known to him. Since the ballades yield, on average, by this method (largely of Dr Seaton's invention) fourteen letters of the alphabet, since there can be any number of 'residual' letters, since the choice of names is wide, since the name need not be complete anyway (though even Dr Seaton hesitates to accept Casdoeas to represent Charles d'Orléans, op. cit., p.7), no wonder that an abundant crop of possibilities turns up! It could not be otherwise. The same scholar has used the same method to attribute to an obscure fifteenth-century figure, Sir Richard Roos, known hitherto only as the translator of Alain Chartier's *La Belle Dame sans merci*, a large part of fifteenth-century English poetry usually attributed to other writers such as Lydgate. (*Sir Richard Roos, Lancastrian poet*, London, 1961. Reviewers, needless to say, have not been kind to this work, see H.S. Bennett in *Review of English Studies*, 13, 1962, pp.174-78, P. Janelle in *Etudes Anglaises*, 14, 1961, pp.232-34.)

Two years later the discovery was announced, by the surrealist poet Tristan Tzara, of a substantial number of secret messages

[15] See above, p.87, on the three poor orphans, or on those responsible for his imprisonment.

in Villon's poetry, but he died before he was able to complete the two volumes he was preparing on the subject (see *28, 43, 30*). Tzara's method resembles that of Seaton but is more sophisticated, choosing letters from a line according to symmetrical patterns round a variable centre. Any single line may offer several anagrams. Thus, we are informed, 'Je laisse, de par Dieu, mon bruit' (*Le Lais*, line 69) contains anagrams of Sarmoie, Denise, Perdrier, Itiers and Noé Jolis! Not surprising after all, with sixteen letters of the alphabet to choose from! The principal arguments on which Tzara's theory rests are that the frequency of anagram occurrence is higher than the statistical probability of their accidental occurrence, and that the method was used by a number of other medieval poets. A very thorough computer-based investigation of these claims has demonstrated that they do not withstand analysis (see *50* and *47*, pp.58-61). What anagrams may appear to be present by this method in the poetry of Villon and his contemporaries are there by chance alone. No doubt it is a pity to spoil the fun, but serious misrepresentation of Villon's text was involved.

And now for the sexual allusions ... For some writers, Villon cannot refer to windows, doors, money, purses, swords, broomhandles or whatever without some eroticism lurking near the surface. Extraordinarily far-fetched notions are at times involved, for example, that 'Pendu soit-il' (*Testament*, line 916) means 'let only a sexually competent, "well hung" man undertake to give Marthe seminal "money"' (see *51*, p.33). Even the *Ballade des dames* is not spared (see *51*, p.45 and *41*, pp.90-92). These literary commentaries, when not preoccupied with sex, are often ingenious and rewarding, but on the matter of possible eroticisms *never noticed hitherto*, are to be read with the greatest caution. Sexual fixations are just as characteristic of our age as embarrassed reticence on the subject was of the Victorian era. We are still suffering from an overreaction to that era, and are too easily influenced by Freudian-based fantasies. From prudery we have moved to prurience, from a dearth to an excess. Villon's age was extremely open about sex, making no attempt to conceal it. (See for example stanza CXI of the *Testament* in which the Orfevre de Boys (a colleague of Perrenet Marchand) receives a hundred cloves of Saracen ginger (an aphrodisiac) to bring together tails and arses, hams and sausages, 'until the milk mounts up to the tits and the blood goes down to the balls'. Nothing veiled about that! Other sexual allusions are not quite so brutally frank, but are obvious enough, e.g. the cruelty of his lady-love means that he will have to 'frapper en un autre coing' (*Lais*, line 32)). Difficulties of interpretation admittedly occur, when a prominent figure who could order Villon's arrest was involved, a circumstance necessitating caution. In such instances it is legitimate to suspect the presence of veiled meanings, for example, Villon's protesting, in connection with the Bishop of Orleans 'Je ne suis son serf ne sa biche' (*Le Testament*, line 12). But it is salutary to remember that even here the recent editors of Villon's poetry, Rychner and Henry, see no sexual innuendo. The surface meaning, the one obviously intended, is forceful enough, as it usually is throughout Villon's poetry. There is no need to be side-tracked into hypothetical secondary meanings which have no more justification than Tzara's anagrams.

But there is more to come ... Villon may not be so much the author, as the first victim, of the *Testament* (see *39*, pp.302-05 and *40*, pp.130-31)! Rather than an autobiography, the *Testament* is a 'judiciary farce', the work of a 'railleur', a court-clerk or group of Burgundian clerks living in Paris and intent on satirising their Parisian colleagues (see *40*, pp.128-29). The work was attributed to François Villon because this name happened to lend itself marvellously to the clerk's 'code' or private language (for this Guiraud relies heavily on W. von Wartburg's massive *Französisches etymologisches Wörterbuch* and juxtaposes meanings from different regions of France and different centuries), as France-hoys-Vill-hon which may be interpreted as the one who 'outrage les paroles françaises prétentieuses' (see *40*, pp.148-49). What that means, and what we are supposed to deduce from it, we are not told. But the name can also be read in eighty-one other ways (see *40*, p.149)! In Guiraud's first work, François Villon meant 'un franc villon de Paris' and since 'franc' gives the idea of belonging to a group (franc-maçon etc.) and 'villon' can mean 'verge', that is, 'rod', 'stem' (see *39*, p.301), the name really meant 'un *enfant* (compagnon) de la

Confrérie des verges de Paris, société des gens qui pratiquent la fellation des testicules' (see *39*, ibid.). However, since Villon describes himself as a 'povre escollier', which suggests 'escollié', 'castrated', his role was 'purement passif'. Sighs of relief! Honorary member only, perhaps? All the names are subjected to a similar syllable-by-syllable scrutiny, with hair-raising results, according to the code whose rules Guiraud sets out at length (see *40*, pp.135-50). It is undeniable that tremendous industry and ingenuity have gone into Guiraud's delvings as into Tzara's very different ones. Each method testifies more to the fertile brain of its twentieth-century inventor than to the medieval texts which they torture so cruelly, each is self-defeating in the number of divergent results it provides, choice inevitably being arbitrary. (Equally ingenious and entertaining, but unacceptable, is the notion that the notorious *Coquillard* Simon Le Double was no other than François Villon (see *27*), entertaining reading, but not to be taken seriously.) Guiraud's starting-point, at least, is valid enough: that the conventional approach, seeing Villon as some sort of nineteenth-century poet four hundred years before his time is absurd. Indeed, it is quite wrong to over-sentimentalise Villon's poetry. He is no languid Romantic tearfully meditating on the transience of love and life. It has been one of the purposes of this commentary to show how Villon's greatest poetry grew out of and was motivated by the particular circumstances of his life (but that does not make of it an autobiography) and was written, not so much in melancholy and nostalgia (though they are not absent), but in a mood of resentment and indignation, beginning in his prison cell, eventually spreading out far beyond these narrow confines.

Relevance

The relevance of Villon to our own unsettled era is quickly stated: protest. Protest against tyrannical authority which can treat a human being like an animal, meting out punishment far harsher than is called for, indifferent as to whether the offender lives or dies. Protest against a society of haves and have-nots, against condemnation of prostitutes and beggars, when life, social conditions, the imperfections of human nature, have brought them to this. Protest against the disloyalty of those who fail to practise what they preach, or who disown friends and relatives in their hour of need. Protest against all life which looks so kindly on some, so indifferently on others; protest against love which promises so much yet cheats and deceives, giving a hundred sorrows for a single pleasure; protest against disease and premature ageing; protest against old age which makes caricatures of us all, leaving us lonely, destitute, living on memories; protest against death which subjects us to appalling agonies and puts an end to even the greatest human beauty and to all human aspirations. Villon knows full well that in the last resort all such protests are futile, death swallows us all whether we like it or not, but, true lyric poet that he was, he has condensed into his terse, hard-hitting lines feelings that are common to us all, feelings that can never be alien because they arise entirely from the human condition, feelings echoed by a poet of our own century:

Do not go gentle into that good night,
Rage, rage, against the dying of the light.

Bibliography

A. BIBLIOGRAPHIES

1. Louis Cons. *Etat présent des études sur Villon* (Paris: Les Belles Lettres, 1936). An account of varying attitudes towards Villon from the sixteenth century to the early twentieth, with chapters devoted to Villon criticism in Spain, Italy, Germany and Britain.
2. Pasquale Morabito. *Bibliografia Villoniana*, the concluding part of Giuseppe Brunelli's *François Villon* (Milan: Marzorati, 1961). A very comprehensive list of books and articles on Villon, year by year, up to 1960.

After 1960 the two standard bibliographies of French literature must be consulted. Both include all books and articles relating to Villon:
3. Otto Klapp. *Bibliographie der französischen Literaturwissenschaft* (Frankfurt: Klostermann, annual publication).
4. René Rancœur. *Bibliographie de la littérature française du moyen âge à nos jours* (Paris: Colin, annual publication until 1980).

B. BACKGROUND

5. Pierre Champion. *François Villon, sa vie et son temps* (Paris: Honoré Champion, 2 vols, 1933). Richly detailed, immensely informative and readable work of a distinguished archivist and scholar.
6. Jean Favier. *François Villon* (Paris: Fayard, 1982). The work of an archivist following in Champion's footsteps, writing in a more popular style on Villon's life and times.
7. Wyndham Lewis, Dominic Bevan. *François Villon, a documented survey* (London: Peter Davies, 1928). A highly coloured, imaginative account of Villon's life and times, but with a fairly sound historical basis.
8. Jean-Claude Muhlethaler. *Poétiques du quinzième siècle. Situation de François Villon et Michault Taillevent* (Paris: Nizet, 1983). Situates Villon within the 'personal poetry' tradition of medieval literature far more precisely than Siciliano, who covers a broader spectrum.
9. Italo Siciliano. *François Villon et les thèmes poétiques du moyen âge* (Paris: Colin, 1934, reprinted 1971). Focusses attention on Villon's debt to his precursors, tracing the history of his various themes over the centuries. Learned yet entertaining and delightful to read.

C. EDITIONS

10. Mary B. Speer. 'The editorial traditions of Villon's *Testament*: from Marot to Rychner and Henry', *Romance Philology*, XXXI (1977), pp.344-61.

11. *François Villon. Œuvres*, edited by A. Longnon and C. Foulet (Paris: Champion, Classiques Français du Moyen Age, 4th edition, 1932). A true 'classic', for long the best edition, now superseded by *20*.

12. *François Villon. Œuvres*, edited by L. Thuasne (Paris: Picard, 1923). 3 vols. Very full notes well worth consulting, but they are sometimes misleading.

13. *Villon. Poésies complètes*, edited by R. Guiette (Paris: Le Livre de Poche, Gallimard, 1964). A good working edition, based on *11*, but notes and glossary are barely adequate, and the spelling of the text has been modernised.

14. *François Villon. Œuvres poétiques*, edited by A. Mary, chronology, preface and index by D. Poirion (Paris: Flammarion, 1965). Includes the poems in thieves' slang, omitted from most editions. Notes are minimal, and the text has been modernised.

15. *Le Testament et Poésies Diverses. François Villon*, edited by B.N. Sargent (New York: Appleton-Century-Crofts, 1967). A reliable edition for students based (five years before *20*) on the best surviving manuscript. Footnotes explain difficult words and allusions.

16. *François Villon. Œuvres. Traduction en français moderne accompagnée de notes explicatives*, by A. Lanly (Paris: Champion, 1969). 2 vols. A literal, line-by-line translation, with an abundance of informative footnotes.

17. *François Villon. Œuvres*, edited by A. Mary, preface, biography and bibliography by J. Dufournet (Paris: Garnier, 1970). Includes the poems in thieves' slang, and gives the text in modernised spelling (cf. *14*). Introduction and notes by Dufournet are very detailed, and deserve a better version of the text.

18. *François Villon. Ballades en jargon (y compris celles du manuscrit de Stockholm)*, edited by A. Lanly (Paris: Champion, 1971). Gives the original text of each ballade, with translation and good explanatory notes.

19. *Villon. Poésies complètes*, edited by P. Michel (Paris: Le Livre de Poche, Librairie Générale Française, 1972). The ballades in thieves' slang are included and copious notes refer to recent research on Villon, sometimes giving too much credence to outlandish interpretations. The text is basically that of *11*, modified in places.

20. *Le Testament Villon*, edited by J. Rychner and A. Henry (Geneva: Droz, 1974). 2 vols: I *Texte*, II *Commentaire*.
Le Lais Villon et les poèmes variés (Geneva: Droz, 1977). 2 vols: I *Texte*, II *Commentaire* (referred to as *20*A, *20*B, *20*C, *20*D). The most authoritative edition currently available.

D. BILINGUAL EDITIONS

21. *The Complete Works of François Villon*, translated with a biography and notes by A. Bonner, introduction by William Carlos Williams (London: Museum Press, 1960). Best of the bilingual editions, though based on the now out-dated *11*. The poems in slang are included, and there is a good set of notes.
22. *François Villon*. Selected poems translated by P. Dale (Penguin Books, 1973, 1978). Contains the *Lais*, the *Testament* and eight of the *Poésies Diverses*. The rhymed translation often departs far from the French.
23. *The Poems of François Villon*. New edition, translated with an introduction and notes by G. Kinnell (Hanover and London: University Press of New England, 1982). Omits the poems in slang, gives a fairly literal translation, with some textual notes and a selected bibliography.

E. CRITICISM

24. Patricia M. Ball. 'Sincerity: the rise and fall of a critical term', *Modern Language Review*, 59 (1964), pp.1-11.
25. André Burger. 'La dure prison de Meung', in *Studi in onore di Italo Siciliano* (Florence: Leo S. Olschki, 1966). 2 vols, pp.149-54.
26. ——. 'L'Entroubli de Villon', *Romania*, 79 (1958), pp.485-95.
27. Jean Deroy. *François Villon coquillard et auteur dramatique* (Paris: Nizet, 1977).
28. Charles Dobzynski. 'Le Secret de Villon', *Lettres Françaises*, (1959), pp.1-4.
29. Jean Dufournet. *Recherches sur le Testament de François Villon* (Paris: Société d'édition d'enseignement supérieur, deuxième série, 1967).
30. ——. 'Tzara et les anagrammes de Villon', *Europe*, (1975), pp.113-14, reprinted as Chapter VIII of *31*.
31. ——. *Nouvelles recherches sur Villon* (Paris: Champion, 1980).
32. ——. 'Villon, le laurier et l'olivier', *Revue des Sciences humaines*, 183 (1981), pp.85-93.
33. John Fox. 'The date and composition of Villon's *Testament*', *French Studies*, VII (1953), pp.310-22.
34. ——. 'A note on Villon's *Ballade des seigneurs du temps jadis*', *Modern Language Review*, 55 (1960), pp.414-17.
35. ——. *The Poetry of Villon* (London: Nelson, 1962), reprinted Greenwood Press, 1976.
36. ——. 'François Villon's fifteenth misadventure', *French Studies*, XXIX (1975), pp.129-36.
37. Jean Frappier. 'Pour le commentaire de Villon, *Testament*, vv.751-52', *Romania*, 80 (1959), pp.191-207.
38. ——. 'Les trois ballades du temps jadis dans le *Testament* de Villon', *Bulletin de la classe des lettres et des sciences morales et politiques* (Académie Royale de Belgique), 57 (1971), pp.316-41.

39. Pierre Guiraud. *Le Jargon de Villon ou le gai savoir de la Coquille* (Paris: Gallimard, 1968).
40. ———. *Le Testament ou le gai savoir de la Basoche* (Paris: Gallimard, 1970).
41. David Kuhn. *La Poétique de François Villon* (Paris: Colin, 1967).
42. Norris J. Lacy. 'Villon in his work: the *Testament* and the problem of personal poetry', *L'Esprit Créateur*, XVIII (1978), pp.60-69.
43. Pierre Le Gentil. *Villon* (Paris: Hatier, 1967).
44. Philippe Ménard. ' "Berte au grant pié, Bietris, Alis" ou la résurgence de la culture épique dans la "Ballade des dames du temps jadis" ', *Romania*, 102 (1981), pp.114-29.
45. Gaston Paris. 'Villoniana', *Romania*, XXX (1901), pp.352-92.
46. Italo Siciliano. 'Sur le *Testament* de François Villon', *Romania*, (1939), pp.39-90.
47. ———. *Mésaventures posthumes de Maître Françoys Villon* (Paris: Picard, 1973).
48. Leo Spitzer. 'Etude a-historique d'un texte: *Ballade des dames du temps jadis*', *Modern Language Quarterly*, I (1940), pp.7-22.
49. Robert Louis Stevenson. 'François Villon, student, poet and housebreaker', in *Familiar Studies of Men and Books* (London: Skerryvore, 1925).
50. Lynn D. Stults. 'A study of Tristan Tzara's theory concerning the poetry of Villon', *Romania*, 96 (1975), pp.433-58.
51. Evelyn Birge Vitz. *The Crossroad of Intentions. A Study of symbolic expressions in the poetry of François Villon* (The Hague — Paris: Mouton, 1974).
52. Teodosio Vertone. *Rythme, dualité et création poétique dans l'œuvre de François Villon* (Rome: Lucarini, 1983).

CRITICAL GUIDES TO FRENCH TEXTS

edited by

Roger Little, Wolfgang van Emden, David Williams

DEPT. French

O.N. 9604

PRICE

ACCN. No. EF 6126

✓